T0207704

TRAVELING
Companion

I Married a Soldier

MARGARET DAVIS LEDFORD

WESTBOW
PRESS®
A DIVISION OF THOMAS NELSON
& ZONDERVAN

WestBow Press books may be ordered through booksellers or by contacting:

WestBow Press
A Division of Thomas Nelson & Zondervan
1663 Liberty Drive
Bloomington, IN 47403
www.westbowpress.com
844-714-3454

ISBN: 978-1-6642-5322-3 (sc)
ISBN: 978-1-6642-5321-6 (hc)
ISBN: 978-1-6642-5323-0 (e)

Library of Congress Control Number: 2022901899

Print information available on the last page.

WestBow Press rev. date: 02/04/2022

PREFACE

Little is written about a soldier's wife. She is not a hero, nor does she claim to be.

She knows when a soldier is given an order it is followed. He packs up and goes. Sometimes his family goes with him, often they are left behind. She prays she will be up to the tasks before her, and she can carry on until her hero returns.

When a soldier dedicates his life in Military service to his country, a certain quality becomes a part of him. It is seldom relinquished. Even after retiring from the military, he is still a soldier at heart. My husband, Joel, was one of these soldiers.

I was his traveling companion. This is my story.

I met Joel when I was fourteen,

My mother and my brother and I moved into the neighborhood where Joel's family lived.

Several teenagers living in the area frequently got together in the afternoon to play baseball. One of the girls refused to play if I was chosen to be on her team. I was not good at sports. My brother, Richard, was too young to play with them. He found his own friends and things to do.

Our house was near the ball field, so I usually sat on my front porch and watched when they played. Sometimes Joel came over to talk with me. Some of the others did also, but Joel was the one who caught my attention. He was always polite, and more mature than many of the others. And he was so good looking. Dark brown eyes, black hair, a dimple in one cheek.

He was in high school and I was in my last year of junior high. We never saw each other at school of course. Sometimes we walked around the neighborhood together or we sat on my front porch and talked.

That summer my family took our yearly trip to the Appalachian Mountains in Virginia to visit my grandparents. While we were there, Joel wrote a letter to me. In that letter he said he had a question to ask me when I came home.

That question was "Will you be my girl?" My mother thought I was too young at fourteen to have a boyfriend who was sixteen.

But a girl could dream.

I began my first year of high school that fall. Joel was two years ahead of me in school. When we got our school yearbooks that year there was nothing about me in the book because I was just a freshman. Something made that book extra special for me.

Joel wrote on the first page of the book, "You are the sweetest girl in the world to me and I will always love you."

He wanted to play on the school football team, but he could not attend after school practice. He had to go to work after school.

So—if you don't practice, you don't play.

He worked at the Blue Bird Ice Company. His job was to make the delicious ice cream the company sold. He and his brother Calvin also sold newspapers and cut grass for neighbors. They worked with a gentleman who was a carrier for the local newspaper. They went to a nearby Army base, Camp Croft, to sell the papers.

The Mess Sergeant sometimes made breakfast for them. When Joel was doing basic training he came in contact with that Sergeant.

Joel decided to change jobs. He went to work in a cotton mill, on the third shift. Going to school and working on the third shift in a cotton mill could certainly keep one busy.

He began thinking about joining the Army. He would become eligible for the draft when he turned eighteen. He did not want to be drafted. He thought his options were better if he enlisted.

He and a friend decided to go and talk to the local recruiter.

They went through the enlistment process. Joel passed all the tests. His friend did not. This apparently gave Joel cause to reconsider. He withdrew his application and they both went back home.

A couple of days later, he and his friend went to town to see a movie. The movie theater just happened to be near the recruiter's office. As they were walking toward the movie theater, the recruiter was walking toward them.

So guess what? Recruiters do have quotas to fill.

The recruiter convinced Joel to reconsider. He personally took him to the processing center, not just the recruiting office, to take care of the details and sign the papers.

Joel joined the United States Army in December 1948 with his mother's signature of permission, two months before his eighteenth birthday. His plan was to pull his tour of duty, then go to college under the GI Bill. After basic training at Fort Jackson, South Carolina, he was allowed a short leave before beginning his new assignment. I thought he would be assigned to Fort Jackson and since we lived in South Carolina he would come home often.

I was mistaken.

He was assigned to the 25th Infantry Division. The 25th Infantry was in Japan. Japan was not close to home. And I did not see him again for more than two and a half years.

Little did I know then what those two and a half years would bring.

The 25th Infantry was part of the American Occupation Forces in Japan with General Douglas MacArthur as Commander. In the summer of 1949, Joel became a vital member of this elite division.

He and I wrote to each other often and I looked forward to receiving those letters. In one of them he wrote, "Don't forget whose sweetheart you are." My answer to that was, "I won't forget."

By late Spring of 1950 I began thinking his deployment should be about finished, and he would be coming home. He had a year and a half remaining on his enlistment and he could be stationed stateside.

It didn't happen that way.

What did happen on June 25, 1950 changed the course of many lives. When the North Korean Army crossed the 38th Parallel that day, the American forces in Japan suddenly acquired an urgent change in assignment. They loaded up and moved out. They were on the way to help the South Korean forces defend their country.

Joel was one if those soldiers. Soon after, he was serving as a mortar squad leader in the southeastern corner of South Korea, facing a fierce enemy. At the age of nineteen, Joel was seriously wounded in combat along the Naktong River near the Puson Perimeter in South Korea.

He was fighting for his life, and he was praying fervently. God heard and answered those prayers. The enemy rifle fire which struck his helmet did not kill him. He was taken to a U.S. Army hospital in Japan to be treated for his injuries and given time to recover before returning home.

He returned to the United States in November 1951, thirty months after leaving. Joel had been handsome as a teenager. Then, at twenty-one, in his Army uniform, Wow! His smile took my breath away.

He was assigned to Fort Bragg, North Carolina. He drove home most weekends. We spent time together on these weekends, reminiscing, getting to know each other again.

This girl's dreams did come true.

Joel and I were married the following year, on September 6, 1952. I was nineteen and Joel was twenty-one. With a short honeymoon trip to the beautiful Blue Ridge Mountains of Tennessee, we began our journey together. This journey has taken us across four continents, several oceans, from the east coast to the west coast of the United States, and to many destinations in between.

I would do it all again if only I could.

1

CHAPTER

Joel enlisted in the army December 28, 1948. He was sent to Fort Jackson, South Carolina, for basic training. He then completed a course in Leadership School. The commanding officer discussed with him the opportunity of continuing on to OCS - Officer Candidate School. Before that could be arranged, he received orders for deployment. The Army apparently had a need for him elsewhere. He was given a short leave before deployment. When he came home, he had a small detail to take care of.

What was he going to do with Trouble?

He had accepted a small dog from a friend who could no longer keep him. Joel's mother did not especially like dogs. Not up close, anyway. As an act of kindness to her son, she agreed to keep Trouble and take care of him. I don't know if she would have admitted it, but I think she learned to love Trouble. He certainly loved her and followed her everywhere.

Joel returned to Fort Jackson and prepared to deploy. This was May 1949. He turned eighteen on March the first of that year. He and a number of other soldiers left South Carolina on a train traveling west. Their destination was San Francisco, California.

They made several stops along the way to pick up other passengers. Joel took pictures when he could. He later sent some of them to me in a letter. He also sent me a handkerchief which had been made from an unusual substance.

In this letter he wrote:

> *"I am sending you a souvenir handkerchief in this letter. An Indian peddler got on the train in California, selling them. I did not believe his story that they were made from cactus fibers. Finally, he convinced me. I bought one for you and one for Mom.*

In May 1949, Joel and the others boarded a ship leaving San Francisco Bay, going under the Golden Gate Bridge into the Pacific Ocean.

**Note: An interesting coincidence about San Francisco and the Golden Gate Bridge - tell you about it later.

They were on the way to Japan. He said this trip was not the most comfortable experience for many of them. A number of those on board were seasick a good portion of the way.

He wrote to me again when he arrived in Japan. It was good to hear from him. I missed him already. Letters were our one and only method of communication. We did not have cell phones, Facebook, E-mail, and other means which we have today.

Joel was assigned to the 25th Infantry Division, 35th Regiment. He would serve as a member of the American Occupation Forces in Japan, under the command of General Douglas MacArthur. His duty station was Otsu, Kyoto, Japan. When they arrived, they were given a small booklet, along with other needed items.

The 25th Infantry Division is known as the "Tropic Lightning" Division. The division shoulder patch is red and gold in color and is in the shape of a "poi" leaf, which grows in abundance in Hawaii where the Division was activated. A jagged streak of gold lightning is in the middle of the patch and represents the familiar name of the division.

The return address on the letters Joel wrote to me those first months in Japan are Co. E 35th Regiment.

I will tell you more about the 25th Infantry "Tropic Lightning" 35th Regiment later in my story. In the meantime, I would like to share some of Joel's letters.

July 12, 1949   *35th Regiment*

Camp Otso, Kyoto, Japan

Darling, I wrote you yesterday that I was going to take part in some sports events today. I played nine games of volleyball. Each team played three games each. We beat two of the teams.

I didn't play this evening. I had work to do and letters to write.

I wish I were home so I could have supper with you.

With all my love always.

August 14, 1949

Darling, I didn't go to chapel service this morning. I got up late and there were several things I had to do.

I received a letter from Mom. She wrote that she was looking for a pocket Bible for me. That was nice of her to think about, but I already have one. I got it at Fort Jackson before I left. If she sends me another one I can give this one to someone else.

August 25, 1949   *Co G Eta Jima*
                                     School Command

Dearest Darling,

I guess you noticed. I am going to school again. I have an address change.

I received two letters from you today. I should have received them before I left the 35th Regiment. You mailed them on August 12 and 13.

Honey, in my school work, I am afraid I am not doing so well, at least not my best.

Today in administrative class I went to sleep a couple of times. The administrator apparently noticed, because he called on me. By the answers I gave, I must have still been asleep.

I may go back into the field, even if the work is harder. I can't see myself as a clerk, can you?

In early September I began my junior year of high school. My classes that year, in addition to math, English, and history, were bookkeeping, typing, and shorthand. Shorthand was interesting and not difficult to learn. I chose those classes because I wanted to prepare to be an accountant after I graduated.

Shortly before school began that year, I had my sixteenth birthday. I was then allowed to work part time. I applied for a job at a bakery in town and I was hired. The bakery was within walking distance of the high school. That was convenient for me.

I worked several afternoons each week and usually a full day on Saturday. It was interesting to see the baking process and to watch the birthday and wedding cakes being decorated. I didn't do any of the baking or decorating. My job was to sell the delicious baked goods.

School had gotten off to a good start. I was comfortable with my classes. The yearbook did have a picture of me that year. I made a dress in economics class. My teacher took a picture of me wearing my dress and she arranged for the picture to be in the yearbook.

I sent a copy to Joel.

My Grandmother Davis taught me how to sew on her sewing machine. As I think about it, I remember she would not allow anyone else to touch that sewing machine. The first thing I made was a cotton skirt. I was so proud of that skirt.

October 30, 1949   *Mount Fugi*

Night before last we had one of the worst storms I have ever witnessed. It was a typhoon.

We were camping at Mount Fugi. Every tent in the regiment blew over or was torn up. About four hundred tents blew over. It was something to see. We moved into a wooden building for the night. As the storm moved out we began putting our tents back together and gathering our equipment.

I took some pictures. I will send you some. Darling, I guess I will sign off for now.

P.S. I love you.

November 5, 1949   *Co. E 35ᵗʰ Infantry*

I received a letter from you today. It helped a little, but I am still lonesome for you.

Honey, thank you for saying that I deserve to be a PFC. I think so too. I guess I will make it soon. I appreciate you writing to me regularly.

Being a squad leader keeps me busy and I have other duties as well. I guess a little extra work won't hurt. Think so? I am pretty lenient with my boys. I am not stubborn with them, but they know better than to give me a hard time.

Honey, I love you very much and I am looking forward to the day we can be together again. Sometimes I could kick myself for joining the army and leaving you.

Be good and be a sweet girl, or maybe I should say, be my sweet girl.

Write to me.

With all my love, always.

December 5, 1949   35th Regiment

OTSU - Japan

Dearest Darling,

We came back from Albino on Saturday. As usual it has taken time to get my equipment cleaned and straightened up. The hard part is we go back tomorrow and will stay until Saturday.

When we do field maneuvers or simulate combat, we always get our clothes dirty and muddy. Weapons usually require a lot of cleaning after being in the field. This is necessary to do the work the Infantry is required to do.

I learned how to dig a fox hole that passed inspection.

Today I had another offer for the supply clerk's job. We are changing supply Sergeants. The one who is taking over wants me to be his clerk. I told him tonight I will think about it. I may take it. I don't know.

Honey, the song, "I Love You So Much it Hurts Me" describes my love for you. If I had you with me now, I believe I would be satisfied, even over here.

Darling, I won't change as far as loving you. My biggest desire is getting home to you.

December 8, 1949   *OTSU*

Honey, my friend Edward will be going home in about a week. I told him that he could stop by to see you and Mom when he gets back to the states.

I have been telling him what a pretty and nice girl I have. He has been a good friend and I can trust him to remember whose girl you are.

January 11, 1950   *OTSU*

Dearest Darling,

I haven't had a chance to write to you for several days. We had a rough week at Albino. Then, I came back to OTSU to find that someone had broken into my locker and stolen my billfold.

In addition to taking all the money in the billfold, they also took my ration card, my birth certificate and pictures. Someone is always taking blankets or wool clothes to sell to the Japanese. I lost a sweater last month. I wish I could catch those thieves.

I was on guard duty last night and most of the day today. I got off about five this afternoon. It was snowing all night and most of the day today. It is not as bad here as it was in Albino, though it gets pretty cold walking guard.

Sweetheart, I guess I will stop for now. Remember that I love you and only you. Be good and write.

With my love always.

January 29, 1950   *OTSU Sunday*
Dearest Darling,

I received a letter from you Friday. I didn't forget to write. I just haven't had a chance.

Honey, if my forgetting you is the only worry you have, you don't have any worries at all.

Darling, the grades you made in history and shorthand are really something to be proud of. I am very proud of my sweetheart, as usual.

Darling, I am glad that the winter at home hasn't been rough this year. I hope it snows just for you.

January 31, 1950   *OTSU*

Dearest Darling,

I received a letter from you today. You mentioned going to church. I haven't been able to go as much as I should.

We are kept busy here, on training missions, going here and there, cleaning equipment after those missions.

I guess that is what the Army does. It gets pretty rough at times. I know this is necessary to do the work the Infantry is required to do. In my way of thinking, the Infantry is the most important component of the army.

We had a big parade this past Wednesday for General Kean, the Division Commander. It was a good parade, everyone said. Being in it, I can hardly say.

Honey, for the past few days, I have been working in the Orderly Room. There is really a lot a person has to know to keep the Orderly Room going.

I hope I know enough to do that and my typing is good enough.

Write often.

With all my love forever.

April 8, 1950

Dearest Darling,

> *I received a letter from you today. Guess what?*
>
> *Today, the Platoon Sergeant said that all of us would get a GI haircut. Naturally I did get it cut.*
>
> *Well, guess it will grow back in a year or so.*
>
> *Not only did we have to get the haircut, we have to starch and iron our work clothes, fatigues. This usually takes about an hour to press and about fifteen minutes to get dirty.*
>
> *I hate to wash and iron clothes, then crawl into a foxhole.*
>
> *Our platoon is the best in the company. It takes a lot of work to prove it to the other platoons.*

School had gone well that year. I liked most of my classes. I think I was not the only one looking forward to summer break.

I was also hoping Joel would be coming home soon. He had been in Japan for a year. Unfortunately, he did not come home that year.

CHAPTER

About a month after school let out, we received devastating news. On Sunday, June 25, 1950, the North Korean military forces launched an attack on South Korea. They crossed the 38th parallel that morning and began forcefully pushing through and moving south.

General Douglas MacArthur, the Supreme Commander of the American Forces in Japan, was notified. He contacted the other Military leaders for a meeting.

The American Military in World War II was the strongest in the world. They had downsized at the end of that war. In 1950, the American Army had ten divisions and eleven separate regiments on active duty. They were missing artillery, tank units, and much more. The greatest weakness was equipment and ammunition. The American forces did not allow that to stop them. They went to the aid of South Korea.

In the first three months of the war, more than one hundred thousand men and nearly two million tons of equipment and supplies arrived. Even with all of this, the American and the South Koreans were being pushed back. The situation was grim.

The North Korean army was thirty-three miles from Pusan and pushing south. General MacArthur drew up a plan. He convinced the other generals, admirals, staff officers, and joint chiefs of staff this was the best choice.

The 25th Infantry Division was pulled out of line in the north and rushed to Masan. They were there in the southeastern corner of South Korea. The entire 25th Division was ashore by July 15, and they launched the first large UN attack on Monday, August 7.

There could be no more pulling back. Any further retreat would lead to disaster, our soldiers drowning in the Sea of Japan. General Walker issued his infamous "Stand or Die" order.

The 25th Infantry began with determination to push the North Koreans back. By using the Naktong river as a barrier, they finally had a defense line. The vital rail line between Pusan and Taejo was never cut by the North Korean forces during the perimeter battle.

On September 7, General Walker proclaimed, "Our lines are holding." There would be many battles ahead, but this was the turning point.

Joel was one of those American 25th Infantry soldiers there in Pusan, along the Naktong River. I didn't hear from him for several weeks. I was thinking about him, as I often did, and wondering why he had not written. A short time later, I learned he was in Korea.

One night an unusual feeling came over me, and I began to cry. I went to bed crying and didn't know why. At times unusual occurrences happen and we can't explain what is causing it. I honestly felt what happened to me that night was telling me something.

A short time later, Joel's mother received a telegram telling her that he had been wounded in battle. A rifle shot struck his helmet and knocked him unconscious. There was a deep indentation in the left side of his helmet, but the bullet did not penetrate the helmet.

I sincerely thank God for that helmet.

When he regained consciousness, only one other member of his squad remained. They had both been injured and needed help. I have often wondered why the other squad members left them behind. They were able to reach shelter and were then taken to the American army hospital in Osaka, Japan.

When Joel was released from the hospital, he was assigned as Assistant NCO of the shipping department. He wrote a letter to me:

October 15, 1950   *Tokyo, Japan*

Dearest Darling,

I got a letter from you today that you wrote on September 26. I am really glad to hear from you.

I received ten letters today and I enjoyed reading all of them. They were all sent to the Osaka hospital. I should still get some that were sent to Korea if they haven't given up trying to find me.

I have been assigned to the shipping department. I am the Assistant NCO. I don't care for the paperwork, but anything is better than Korea. We have a lot of men coming in from the States. What we could have done with these troops back in July.

We process all of those coming in and also those from the hospitals. Most of them will be going to Korea. We see that they have equipment, and let them zero their rifle. We see that they have insurance or let them make out an allowance.

A lot of paperwork is involved. Darling, be good and write often.

With all my love.

October 20, 1950　　　　　　　*Camp Drake, Japan*

Dearest Darling,

I got a letter from you yesterday and I was very glad to hear from you. It was the letter you wrote after you heard I was wounded.

I had a problem for a while, not speaking coherently, and my memory was affected. I even forgot my serial number. I'll bet you don't forget my serial number as often as you have written it.

I went to Tokyo yesterday to see the Bob Hope show. After standing in line for about eight blocks long, I did get to see the show and even found a seat. The theater seats about 3,500 and it was really crowded. All in all, the show was good and it was worth the trouble. I sure wish you could have been with me to watch the show.

The company commander wants me to work in the shipping department. There is a lot of paperwork in processing troops and this is my first experience in this work. Really, though, I guess this is the easiest job I have had since being in the army. Guess I better stop and get a little shut-eye. These people have a hard time waking me up in the mornings. Sleeping so much in the hospital got to be a habit.

I love you very much.

October 27, 1950   *Camp Drake*

Dearest Darling,

I was on orders to be transferred to the other side of the camp a few days ago. The company commander asked that my name be taken off the order and I remain here.

This suits me fine. I am tired of changing homes every few days. The next place I want to go is the states. Darling, I love you very much.

Be good and write often.

November 1, 1950

Dearest Darling,

I received two letters from you yesterday. The letters did not have to go all over the place like some of the others have done.

I have gained some weight. Since we have changed mess halls, we have had good meals.

Darling, guess I will stop for now. I love you very much and I hope it won't be long until I come home.

November 19, 1950   *Camp Drake*

Dearest Darling,

I got a letter from you today and I was very glad to hear from you. I will try my best to get the letter answered tonight. Every time I sit down, somebody always comes in and bothers me.

I have changed jobs again. My duty now is Charge of Quarters. I like this job better than the last one. I stay here in the Receiving Office. I have quarters here. I have an assistant and he has his quarters here also.

We receive men now rather than shipping them. They have been arriving here all day. We give them bedding and assign them to a room. We also issue ration cards and we get information so as to be able to keep a roster of those coming in.

My former company commander and battalion commander were wounded about the same time that I was. They both came through, being processed to go back to Korea.

Sweetheart, think I will stop writing for now and try to catch a few winks before breakfast. Be good and write often.

With all my love.

November 24, 1950

Dearest Darling,

I haven't received a letter from you since I wrote to you last, but I did get a very nice Christmas card from you yesterday.

We shipped about forty men on Thanksgiving Day. All of them have already been to Korea. Many of them have been wounded and now going back.

I am Charge of Quarters tonight and I am getting sleepy already. I will have the day off tomorrow. Maybe I can catch up on my sleep.

I may go to Tokyo tomorrow and pick up a couple of things to send home. How would you like to have a Japanese kimono?

I will stop writing for now and make a round of the barracks to see if everything is ok. Here, anything can happen.

I love you very much.

November 27, 1950

Dearest Darling,

Thought I would write a little tonight. Or maybe I should say early morning. It is now about 2 am.

I have been up the bigger part of the night trying to get some of the work done so as to have things pretty straight for tomorrow. If I stay up much longer I may as well stay up the rest of the day.

I met a guy today who was with me in Korea. He was wounded after I was and now he is going back to Korea. I have seen a number of men who were in my company. I am glad to see them and talk with them about things that happened in the company after I left.

I read a piece in the paper tonight about a Battalion of the 25th Division that is surrounded and they have not been able to get supplies.

Sweetheart, I sure wish I could make it home for Christmas this year and be able to keep that date with you on New Years Eve. I remember when I saw you last and I wonder if you have changed. I think I will be able to recognize you. Think so?

I haven't changed any that I know of other than being a nervous wreck and having a few gray hairs. No, I don't have any gray hairs, yet. If I stay over here much longer I probably will obtain some. Just think, it won't be too much longer until I will be twenty years old and I don't feel over 30. That isn't too bad though, considering I have been in the Infantry for a couple of years.

You said that you think what I have learned in the Army is more than I would have learned in school. I agree with you to a certain extent, but I have forgotten a lot since I was wounded. When I got to where I could talk a little, I still couldn't remember a lot of things. Really, I had it pretty hard for a while, remembering how words were spelled and names of people I didn't know well. It is hard to explain the way I felt when I tried to say something and it just would not be what I was trying to say half the time.

Thankfully, I am getting better. Darling, it has been a long time since I have seen you. For the past several months, I have been looking forward to this month (November) to be sent back to the states, and I would be with you again. As it stands now, I have no idea when I will be sent home.

Please continue to write often and love me.

With all my love.

December 3, 1950

Dearest Darling,

I will write a little tonight before trying to get some sleep. I was expecting men to come in for processing tonight. So far none have arrived. As sure as I go to bed, they will come and probably have a hard time waking me up.

Take care of yourself and be good.

With all my love always.

December 15, 1950

Dearest Darling,

I got a letter from you today and was very glad to hear from you. I got the cake you sent. Thank you for sending it. I am sure the guys will want to share it.

The person who was helping me has gone to Korea. I have a Sgt. who helps me now, but he will probably leave for Korea soon.

Sweetheart, I would like more than anything to be home for Christmas. I guess it just wasn't meant to be. Hearing Christmas carols and seeing Christmas decorations makes me homesick, especially the songs. I would rather not hear them.

Well, maybe I will be home next year for Christmas. At least I hope so. We have received a number of men tonight and we are expecting more. It will be a long night.

With all my love, always.

December 20, 1950

Dearest Darling,

I received a letter from you today and was very glad to hear from you and that you are well and of course that you still love me.

Congratulations on making straight A's on your report card. That is something to be proud of. I am proud of you. Think you can finish the year with nothing but A's?

Darling, as long as I am in this place I doubt that I will make Sergeant. I guess I will have to be satisfied for the time being. If I had stayed in Korea a while longer I would have been promoted. I was the squad leader. Most of the squad leaders were promoted to Sergeant shortly after I was wounded.

I have talked with a number of the men who were in the 35th Regiment with me in Korea and they have come through here. I hated to hear that the 35th had been hit so hard.

Take care of my sweetheart and don't forget that I love her.

December 27, 1950

Dearest Darling,

I hope you had a good Christmas. I had to work Christmas night, which did not surprise me. I didn't mind it much. All the days are about the same here. As you probably know, I was supposed to become a civilian today. These people have other plans for me.

I told the First Sergeant I was out of the army today. Of course, he didn't agree with me. He knew I was only joking with him. I am in the process of reenlisting for another three years. I will have five years in the army when I am twenty-three years old.

By the way, it won't be long until I am twenty years old. Getting to be an old man, aren't I?

Honey, it doesn't seem almost five years ago that I met you. This coming July will make it five years ago that I first saw the girl that I have loved ever since. It was hard for me to realize the fact that we were both young and we still are, but I know that you are the girl for me.

Take care of yourself and write to me.

With all my love always.

January 5, 1951   *Battery A*

1st Artillery Brigade

Camp Drake, Japan

Dearest Darling,

I hope you had a nice New Year's Day and this year will be very good to you. Did you make a New Year's resolution? I went over to the recruiting office yesterday to reenlist. I will have to wait about three more days until I finish my physical examination and my blood test comes back.

Honey, I will write again soon. I love you very much.

January 16, 1951   *Company B*

Special Training BN

R&R Program

Dearest Darling,

As you have probably noticed, I have changed addresses again. I will be expecting an invitation to attend commencement exercises, but as usual I doubt that I will be there.

Do you think you could make all A's if I were there to keep you up late every night?

February 7, 1951

Dearest Darling,

I received a letter from you today. I will do my best to answer it before the men start returning from leave. They begin coming in by the 20s and 30s, which makes my work steady for a few hours.

Darling, thank you for your interest in my health. The question about whether I feel as good as I did before going to Korea is a hard one to answer. I don't exactly know myself. I know that going to Korea did not help any at all. Other than being wounded, the weather, filth, sweat, many miles of walking with a heavy load.

Sweetheart, I love you very, very much. Too much for me to be so far away from you for so long.

May 6, 1951

Darling,

You remember my dog, Trouble? He is still at home and Mom says he is still mean and is always getting into some kind of trouble.

I guess he takes his meanness from me. Think so?

May 24, 1951

I got your letter yesterday and was very glad to hear from you as always. I guess I can't make it home for commencement unless they fly me home in a fast jet plane.

Darling, it was pretty hard for me to decide what to send you for a graduation present. I sent you a watch. Hope I did not make a bad choice. (Note: It was a beautiful watch and I still have it.)

When I come home I will need to look into buying a car. Maybe I could use you as a reference to my character. Would you vouch for me? - Just kidding. It has been so long since I have driven. I may need to learn all over again.

I have an appointment with a board of doctors tomorrow or the next day. I had a check up about three months ago. Now, I have to do it again.

Darling, I will stop for now. It is about my bed-time. Hoping to hear from you again soon.

With all my love.

June 9, 1951

Dearest Darling,

I received your letter of the 4th today and was very glad to hear from you.

Darling, I think you did very good in the test for a scholarship even though you didn't win. Even qualifying to enter the test was something to be proud of. Being fourth was more than something to be proud of.

Anyway, I am so proud of you. You told me one time you would let me be your secretary if I learned

*shorthand. With you being my teacher, I couldn't keep
my mind on shorthand.*

June 17, 1951

Dearest Darling,

*I have been thinking of you all day today (Sunday)
and decided to write to you before going to bed. These
twenty-five months haven't been easy for me, thinking
of you and being kept over here much longer than I
had thought I would be. I have no idea as to when I
will get home.*

*I am looking forward to when that day will come
and I will be with you again.*

With all my love.

July 11, 1951   *Camp Drake*

Dearest Darling,

*Sure was glad to get your letter yesterday. I didn't
get a chance to answer until today. We worked until
five am this morning getting all the men processed and
on their way back to Korea.*

*I don't usually work much at night now but due
to losing two or three regular cadre and having a big*

shipment on top of that we all had to pitch in and get the men processed. I don't have to work tonight, so maybe I can get a good night's sleep.

I believe I will make it home soon, but I couldn't make a guess as to when.

Darling, how are my chances to make a date ahead of time for the day I get home?

Thinking of you. Love, always.

August 20, 1951

Dearest Darling,

I received your letter of the 13ᵗʰ yesterday. I haven't had a chance to answer before now. I am on duty tonight, but most of the men leaving today have been processed. I may be able to get some sleep.

Love you always.

September 27, 1951   *Camp Drake*

Dearest Darling,

I am always glad to get your letters. I am sorry I have waited so long to answer. I hurt my finger trying to put one of these R&R men to bed. He was drunk and he was not very cooperative. It was kind of hard to write with a bandage on my finger. Most of those coming through are cooperative, but now and then we have someone who gives us a problem.

I think it was a mistake for President Truman to relieve General MacArthur of his command. He was well liked by the Japanese and South Korean people. He has proven himself to be a smart man.

General MacArthur was like President Roosevelt. He was capable of gaining power and he wasn't afraid of it.

Honey, I love you very much and I can truthfully say that you are the only girl I love.

Hope to hear from you again soon.

September 29, 1951
Dearest Darling,

I received your letter yesterday. I didn't get a chance to answer it last night. We had a busy night with a number of men coming through to be processed.

With the Company Commander we have now there isn't much chance of a promotion. He seems to like me and is satisfied with my work, but he has never recommended anyone for promotion.

I don't plan to make the Army my career and hope I won't have to.

When I finish this enlistment, I will be old enough to vote. Think I will be qualified to vote by then?

Hope to see you soon. I love you very much.

October 21. 1951

Darling, I hope I will be sent home by air when I leave here. I don't care for another boat ride. Maybe I will be home by Christmas

All my love.

3
CHAPTER

Joel returned home the week of Thanksgiving 1951, after being away from home for two and a half years. His family gathered for dinner to welcome him home. He called me, then borrowed his brother-in-law's car and came to see me. He would be home on a forty-five day leave before reporting for duty.

He knew that he needed transportation and he began looking into the possibility of buying a car if he could find one he could afford on an Army Corporal's pay. His mother had a pleasant surprise for him. He had money in the bank of which he had no knowledge.

When he received orders for Japan, he arranged for an allotment to be sent each month to his mother. He intended this money for her use. She had placed almost the entire amount in the bank for him. He had not even considered the possibility of buying a new car. But, that is exactly what he did. He bought a new car. His mother's thoughtfulness and generosity was an encouragement for him to be more careful how he spent his money, and to save as much as possible.

It was so good to have him home. It had been a long two and a half years. He came to visit me in the evening. We sat and talked, walked around the neighborhood, just spent time getting to know each other again. He had been away for so long, been through so much, then wondering where his next duty station would be. South Carolina would be his processing center. There was a possibility he could be stationed there, but probably not likely.

He knew I had dated in high school. One evening he asked, "Are you going to be dating any of those other boys? Because I am not interested in sharing."

My answer was, "No, never again."

Joel met the person I had been dating. He said, "Darling, I don't know why, but after I got home, I am not very jealous of him."

When his leave time was up, he reported to Fort Jackson, South Carolina to begin processing for his next assignment. He wrote me a note.

January 5, 1952

Dearest Darling,

I made the trip in about an hour and a half. I will begin processing this week. I sure wish I could have brought you with me.

All my love always.

January 7, 1952   Fort Jackson, South Carolina

Dearest Darling,

We began processing today. It will probably take a week. This morning we took our mental and qualifying tests. Believe it or not, I beat the score I made when I came in the Army. I was given the opportunity again to go to OCS, but I declined the offer. I have been a Corporal so long now. It would be hard for me to give it up. Maybe I will make Sergeant. I have been ready and waiting since Korea.

Don't forget whose sweetheart you are.

With all my love.

January 13, 1952   *Fort Jackson*

Dearest Darling,

I have processed all week. Next I will go for an interview and they will determine where to send me. That decision will come from Washington.

Hope to see you soon.

January 28, 1952   *Fort Jackson*

Dearest Darling,

I went in this morning to ask why it is taking so long. They told me not to worry about it and to stop pestering them. It is a good thing I didn't tell that Sergeant what I wanted to tell him. I would have said something that put me in trouble.

January 29, 1952   *Fort Jackson*

Darling, I got my orders today. I am being sent to Fort Bragg, North Carolina. I will leave some time tomorrow. Fort Bragg is not as far away as some of the other Army bases I could have been sent to.

Bad news - I won't get Saturday off. I can't leave the post. I guess I will spend Washington's birthday washing my car.

With all my love always.

March 8, 1952

Darling,

I have CQ Charge of Quarters tomorrow. I won't be able to see you this weekend. We have processed eighty men for shipment to Korea this week. My prayers go with them.

I love you very much.

Joel and I continued to write to each other. He came home on the weekend as often as he could.

I changed jobs. I had been working at a finance company since I graduated. The manager of a different finance company offered me a position I accepted for several reasons. It was interesting to learn more about the finance business, the accounting and bookkeeping process. I liked the work I was doing and I was thankful for those classes in high school.

When Joel came home on the weekend, we usually went to church on Sunday morning. One Sunday we drove to the mountains.

We took my mother and Joel's mother. Also a picnic lunch. Joel and I took off our shoes and went wading in the stream, thankful to be together.

We treasure precious moments, don't we?

Sometimes on the weekend we went to a movie, to a drive-in restaurant, or just out to get ice cream. The drive-in restaurant we most frequently went to was called The Beacon. That was where he gave me an engagement ring. In the car, in The Beacon parking lot.

CHAPTER

We decided on a date for the wedding. Joel was given a three-day pass. My office manager gave me the week off. We were married on Saturday afternoon, September 6, 1952.

I had reserved a time with our Pastor at the parsonage and with a photographer. I left work about noon. I then went to the florist to pick up my corsage, to the bakery to pick up the wedding cake, then home to finish packing.

Joel came home to get ready. He had not even told his mother we were getting married. He came to pick up my mother, my brother, and me. My Aunt Claudia and Uncle Woodie met us at the parsonage.

We were married in a simple ceremony. We then returned home

where family members came for a short celebration. We then began our journey to the beautiful Blue Ridge Mountains.

The area of South Carolina where our families live is referred to as the foothills of the mountains. Upon leaving our home in South Carolina, then driving northwest, one can see the mountains in the distance.

We left home and began traveling northwest. We stopped in Tryon, North Carolina to spend the night.

On Sunday, we went to a local restaurant for an early lunch before continuing to Tennessee. The name of the restaurant was Caro-Mi. It was located beside a small stream. A large porch with chairs gave customers the opportunity to sit, relax, watch the water tumble over the rocks and flow by.

An interesting coincidence is that the Caro-Mi and The Beacon are both in operation today.

Leaving Tryon, we continued on to Cherokee, North Carolina, stopping to have a look at many interesting and historic things, and buy a small souvenir. The Blue Ridge Parkway took us through the Blue Ridge Mountains toward Gatlinburg, Tennessee. The leaves had begun to change colors, shades of yellow and orange beginning to show.

Something else interesting showed up. Two bears were wandering around on the side of the road. We slowed to watch them. They checked us out, then wandered off. No bother to us in any way.

We reached Gatlinburg, an interesting town to wander around and explore. On Monday we began our way back home. The three-day pass went by too quickly.

On our way we stopped in North Carolina at Lake Junaluska. We walked around a portion of the lake on a walkway lined with beautiful rose bushes in full bloom of varying colors. A large white cross stood on the mountain across from the lake. It was beautiful to see.

We came home Monday evening, then left Tuesday morning, going to Fort Bragg. I had the remainder of the week off from work, but Joel's three-day pass had expired. We checked in the post guest house. The first morning there I was awakened by an unaccustomed sound.

Reveille.

Fort Bragg is adjacent to Fayetteville, North Carolina. I didn't see much of either during the short time I was there. Before the 1940s, Fayetteville was a small textile town. Fort Bragg became a training camp for soldiers and grew from five thousand troops in 1940 to more than one hundred thousand at the beginning of World War II. Before Pearl Harbor, Fayetteville had fewer than eighteen thousand residents. As Fort Bragg grew in size and number, Fayetteville grew also.

Joel brought me home on Saturday. We decided I would stay at home and continue working and saving as much of my salary as possible. That plan lasted three weeks. I quit my job, packed my bag, and caught the bus.

Joel was waiting for me at the bus station. We checked in the post guest house again and began looking for a place to live. We found a room for rent, with an arrangement to share the bathroom and kitchen with the owner.

That arrangement didn't last long.

The owner was bossy. She didn't say anything to my husband. She fussed at me when he wasn't there. She complained that we used too much water, we stayed in the kitchen and the bathroom too long. We were not allowed to sit in her living room in the evening. She wanted us to stay in our little room and not bother her. She didn't want us there, but she didn't want to be alone. Her sister came to visit and she apologized for the way the owner was treating us.

One night my husband and I were going to a drive-in movie. She insisted on going with us and she sat in the back seat of the car.

We moved out at the end of the month.

We found a small house for rent near the Army base. The house had three rooms - a bedroom, bathroom, and kitchen. All were adequately furnished to meet our needs. The house was in the owner's back yard. They were kind, generous, friendly people. They seemed to appreciate having us there and they offered any assistance we needed. They allowed us the use of their washing machine. Then I hung the clothes on the outside lines to dry.

I learned how to wash, starch, and iron those khaki uniforms until they could almost stand alone.

We settled in our little house. Joel called it our "chicken coop."

I began looking for a job. I found one fairly quickly, another accounting position. I went to work at the Public Works in Fayetteville. The Public Works offices were in the same building as the city jail. A lot of things happened there. I wish I could tell you about some of those.

Our house was near a bus stop. It was convenient for me to take the bus to work and back.

Joel drove to the Army post. He had to be there really early. That took a little getting used to for me. I didn't know the Army kept such early hours. I wasn't accustomed to getting up at that time in the morning. I discovered there were a number of things I needed to learn about being a soldier's wife.

A soldier must be strong, resourceful, dependable, and obedient.

His duty is not to question, but to follow orders and complete the mission.

A soldier's wife must be strong and dependable also. She must learn to deal with the hardships that may come with periods of separation by determination and perseverance. At times it may not be easy to do, but she can hold things together and make major decisions on her own when necessary. How a soldier's wife conducts herself reflects on her husband and on the Army as well.

I didn't feel threatened by any aspect of the Army. I may have at times felt a bit overwhelmed. And I knew I had a lot to learn as we began our life together. I was pleased to be called an Army Wife.

Joel was assigned to the 20th Engineer Battalion. That kept him busy. I was comfortable in my work and I was getting used to the Army time schedule. We drove home to visit family as often as we could.

After several months, Joel's discharge date was drawing near. I began thinking about moving back home, but I knew that might not be a certainty. Joel was seriously considering reenlisting. I understood why this was important to him. He was a Soldier. He was a teenager when he began this journey. Now he was five years older and a mature adult.

A portion of time along this journey had been served in combat. This was not something that would easily vanish from his thoughts.

Also, what kind of work did he want to do if he came back home? He had completed one year of college during the time he had been in the Army, but he had not chosen a specific career to pursue. He could continue in college but was that what he wanted to do? Also, he had been promoted to Sergeant. That was important to him. He had worked hard to achieve that.

So, after serious consideration, reenlisted for another three years.

His mother didn't have to give her written permission this time.

Shortly after reenlisting, he decided to make other changes as well. He began his service in the Infantry. Then he became a Supply Sergeant.

Now he decided he wanted to become a Career Counselor (Recruiter). He was assigned to learn how to be a Recruiter. He then served at Fort Bragg for several months, convincing young Soldiers to stay in the Army, to reenlist. He also counseled those who came on post to get information about enlisting. He explained to them the benefits and the opportunities they could experience.

After several months in this position at Fort Bragg, Joel was re-assigned, again. This assignment was the recruiting office in Marion, North Carolina.

Time to pack our bags and get on the road again.

5

CHAPTER

W e began our drive west across North Carolina. As we were getting close to Marion, we took a short side trip.

He drove me to my mother's house to stay a few days. He went on to Marion to report in and to look for an apartment to rent. Someone introduced him to a gentleman who owned an apartment building as well as a furniture store. An apartment was available and the kind gentleman provided the furniture items we needed, and an affordable rent agreement.

Joel accepted his offer. He came to get me and we moved in. The apartment was comfortable and not quite as small as the little house in Fayetteville.

The recruiting office was in the Marion Post Office building.

Each of the military branches maintained offices there. The recruiters then traveled to other towns throughout the area. Office space was available for them on a regular schedule. Joel began his duties to encourage young people to become Soldiers.

In addition to his office space in Marion and other towns, he visited schools to meet with prospects. He even ventured into corn fields, tobacco fields, and other farmlands to talk with young people working there, convincing them the United States Army could offer something better. If they needed transportation, he brought them to the bus station and sent them on the way to begin basic training.

I began checking around to see what kind of work I could do. I met the local librarian who lived in the apartment building. She offered me a job and I accepted. Though it was not accounting, it was a good opportunity for me. The library was near the apartment building, easily within walking distance.

I have always loved books. Working with them was interesting and informative. Getting to know the Dewey Decimal system was not difficult. It was nice to meet and talk with people coming in the library, assist them in choosing a good book to read or study. Several days a week I rode with another librarian in the bookmobile. She and I traveled to different scheduled locations throughout the area so people could check out books. They seemed to be pleased to be able to borrow books when it may not have been convenient for them to travel to the library.

If anyone had a special request, we searched for the book and brought it to them the next time we came to their bookmobile stop.

Joel and I enjoyed exploring the mountains together. We drove around the area on the weekends. He showed me the recruiting locations in the different towns he visited.

Something was usually blooming - spring, summer, or fall. The trees were beautiful in the fall with varying shades of yellow and orange. The mountains were interesting.

Thinking about traveling, I remember I had traveled to the mountains in Virginia with my mother and brother many times to visit my grandparents. My mother was born in Virginia. She moved to South Carolina when she was a teenager and went to work in a cotton mill. That is where she met the man she married. He was also working in the cotton mill.

My mother married my daddy when she was fourteen years old. I have their marriage license to prove it. She was seventeen when I was born. My brother, Richard, was born four years later.

Each day, every moment, we should treasure and appreciate the blessings in our lives instead of thinking and wondering what could have been. My mother was certainly a blessing. She took care of my brother and me when she was barely more than a child.

I got off track there. Let's get back to Marion.

Joel enjoyed fishing and hunting, depending on the season, when he had the opportunity. I sometimes went with him. I took a book to read while he fished. Hunting was not for me. I left that totally up to him.

Nearby, Lake James was his favorite fishing spot. Hunting was somewhere in the mountains.

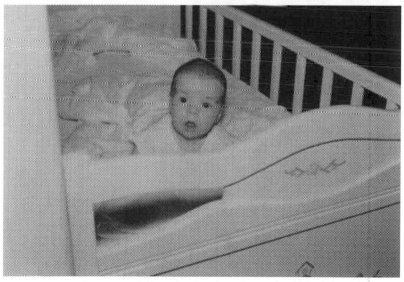

A national magazine, Popular Science, did a full page story, including photographs, of Joel and one of his recruits.

Charlotte, North Carolina was the Recruiting Main Station (RMS) for the area Joel served. He went there for meetings about once a month. He received the Outstanding Recruiting Award for Charlotte RMS in June 1958.

We had been in Marion about two years when our first baby was born. I quit my job at the library a few months before her birth. We were so happy to have her on the way. We went to the furniture store to pick out a baby bed and found the prettiest little pink one for her. When Joel went back to pick up the bed, the owner gave him the mattress for it.

I woke up one morning with an unusual feeling. I called the doctor, and he said, "No, probably not yet." Joel had a meeting scheduled at the Charlotte office. I told him to go to the meeting. I would be alright.

He gave me the phone number of the Charlotte office if I needed to call him. A short time later, I decided it was time to make that call. A neighbor across the hall took me to the hospital. Joel reached Charlotte, then turned around and came back. He made it to the hospital before our baby was born.

When we came home from the hospital, Joel's mother came for a few days, then my mother came. We appreciated their help. Maybe they enjoyed spending time with their grandbaby. Think so?

When Debra began moving around more and more in her bed, she seemed to notice her daddy's dress blue jacket, which was on a hanger over the door near her bed. She probably noticed the medals more than the jacket. One of those was the Purple Heart.

We had been in Marion for about three years when Joel received orders to return to Fort Bragg. We moved into post housing. The apartment was adequately furnished. Living on post was convenient with access to the PX and commissary, medical needs if required. The PX is the post exchange, similar to a CVS or Walmart. The commissary is the grocery store.

Debra and I went to watch a parade one day. The parade field was within walking distance. I pushed her in her stroller. Her daddy was a member of the Honor Guard and he carried the American flag. She was too little to remember, but I do.

Winter came and brought snow. Debra loved when Daddy brought her outside all wrapped up in her yellow snowsuit to play in the snow. We didn't receive snow often. It was a treat when it came.

Joel began thinking about changing his MOS (Military Occupation Specialty) again. He was interested in STRAT COMM-Strategic Communication Command. After some research, he requested a transfer. His request was granted. He received orders for Fort Monmouth, New Jersey.

Marion was a short distance from home, Fort Bragg was a little further, Fort Monmouth was much farther away. Little did I know then the distance this duty change would bring.

The rest was yet to come.

We began our drive North. I had traveled to Tennessee and Virginia, but never as far north as New Jersey. We carried our basic needs in the car. Movers brought everything else. Fortunately, military bases have guest facilities available for incoming military with accompanying dependents.

Post housing was not available for us. We began looking for a place to live. We found an apartment near the base. It was on the second floor with a private outside entrance, and was furnished with most of what we needed. One item we did buy was a chest for Debra. Her daddy painted the chest white and the knobs on the drawers pink. He also bought a small mirror which had a wood casing around the mirror and the base. He painted the wood parts pink. He positioned the stand on top of the chest at just the right height for her to see into it. She then had a chest to match her bed.

We met some of the other residents of the apartment building.

Debra's second birthday was coming up. We arranged a small party for her and invited three children who were about her age to share birthday cake and ice cream with her.

Joel had a busy schedule. In addition to his daytime duties, he had classes to attend several evenings each week. I knew basically what he did as an Infantryman, a Supply Sergeant, and Career Counselor.

When he transferred to STRAT COM, all I knew was that it involved electronics and communication. I had no idea where this would take us, but I was about to find out.

After several months at Fort Monmouth, Joel received transfer orders. It was time to move again.

CHAPTER

T his time our move was not just across the state or a bit further north. Joel's transfer was to Kagnew Station, an American military base in Asmara Eritrea Ethiopia.

All I knew about Ethiopia was that it is located in the northwest section of Africa and Haile Selassie was the ruler at that time. I didn't know the American Military maintained a base there. Again - there were still a lot of things I didn't know about the American Army. And frankly, many I would never know.

Movers came to pack for us. We drove home to South Carolina for a short visit with our family and to tell them of the new assignment.

Compared to the distance between home and Marion or

Fort Bragg or Fort Monmouth this distance was unexpected and unimaginable.

We began our drive north to New York, stopping to leave our car with the port authority where it would be loaded onto a ship and transported for us. After an overnight stay in New York, the next stop was La Guardia Airport to continue our journey. A journey to a place far away that we knew little about.

This was to be my first airplane trip. Talk about venturing into the unknown, this was way out there.

We boarded the plane with ninety service men and a small number of dependents. We left La Guardia at night, which was probably a good thing. Debra was able to sleep and become comfortable with the airplane. Probably good for me, also.

Our first refueling stop was in Nova Scotia. We were unable to see much since it was dark. We had only a short stop to refuel, therefore we didn't get off the plane.

We continued on across the Atlantic Ocean toward Shannon, Ireland. I remember seeing beautiful green countryside, white sheep grazing peacefully as we came in to land. We left the plane briefly but did not have the opportunity to explore. We got back on the plane, on to our destination. We still had a long way to go.

Our next stop was Frankfurt, Germany. We had a one day

lay-over there, so we checked in the post guest house. Debra had developed a fever and wasn't feeling well. We took her to see a doctor on post. He gave her penicillin, which we discovered did not agree with her. She began the journey feeling well. Now, our little girl was sick. I tried to keep her as comfortable as possible.

We didn't see much in Germany while we were there in Frankfurt, but the view over the Alps as we continued our journey was breathtaking. The mountains were tall, beautiful, and majestic.

Our next stop was Athens, Greece. Joel and some of the others got off the plane for a look around. Our little girl and I remained on the plane. She was asleep as were some of the others. It was night time again.

It had been a long journey since our departure from New York. Our destination was still many miles and hours away. Though Debra didn't feel well, she had been such a good little traveler. She was able to sleep during the night and nap at times during the day. Other times she played with her toys and looked at her books. The flight attendant brought her a treat now and then.

By the time we approached Ethiopia, it was daylight. As the plane began to descend, we looked out the windows with anticipation. Much of what we saw was trees, no signs of habitation.

As the plane slowly descended and we came closer to our

destination, we could see there was a city, an airport, a military base, people. This was to be our home for the next two and half years. Of utmost importance, I was here with my husband, and our little girl was here with her daddy.

A sergeant from the Kagnew Station Army Base met us at the airport. He helped us gather our luggage and took us to a hotel, The Hamasien. Interesting that I can remember the name after all this time. It was a comfortable, well equipped hotel, completely adequate for our needs. A horse and carriage waited outside.

The driver was there, waiting to provide a ride wherever one may need to go. Taxies and buses were available, but the horse and carriage arrangement was interesting.

We were to stay at the hotel until we found a house to rent.

The American military base was well equipped with a hospital, commissary, chapel, PX, gas station, and school for children. On post quarters were available for unaccompanied service men and women, but there was limited housing for those with families. Our name went on a long waiting list.

Several American families were staying at The Hamasien while they looked for a place to rent. With the help of the Sergeant who met us at the airport, we found a house in an area called Casabonda.

We were about to discover living in Ethiopia to be uniquely different from what we were accustomed to in the United States.

Casabonda was an elevated section of the city. From our back yard we had a good view of a large portion of the city below and around us. The yards for many of the houses in the neighborhood were surrounded by brick fences and gates with locks. The people in the house next door had a gazelle in their yard. Thank goodness for the fence and the lock.

The car garage in our yard was almost deep enough. Our American car didn't quite go all the way into the opening. It's length extended a few inches.

An American Army family lived in the house across the street from us. They had three children, though they were older than Debra and they all went to school. She sometimes stayed by the fence gate and watched the bus pick up those children for school. She was probably wishing she could go with them. Usually she had only Mommy to play with unless Daddy was home. She loved books and having them read to her. Sometimes we walked around the neighborhood and felt comfortable doing that.

Joel decided to plant a garden to grow flowers and a few vegetables. The weather was warm, a good growing temperature. The flowers were beautiful and the vegetables did well. I remember the dahlias especially. My grandmother grew dahlias, but I had never seen any as tall and beautiful as those Joel grew in that little space. Debra enjoyed playing in the yard and helping Daddy.

A young man, Kadoni, came by each day to do yard work or whatever we needed him to do. One day a large swarm of locusts flew in and tried to descend on the flowers and vegetables. Kadoni ran around the yard with his arms raised, flapping towels in the air and forced the locusts to leave. He was able to prevent the locusts from devouring our garden. Kadoni was determined to not allow that to happen.

A young lady, Sarah Danielle, came to work for us. She did the cleaning and the laundry. She and Kadoni both spoke English well. Some things they said were a little different. The first day she came, I asked her how she got there. There was no indication of transportation. She said, "by my feet." I had not had a maid or yard boy before. Sarah and Kadoni were both willing to do whatever we asked them to do. Sarah went to the Coptic Church. I don't know about Kadoni.

We went to the chapel on post. Debra liked the Sunday school class and the papers she was given to bring home. One day she was standing by the front gate in our yard. Some children stopped and wanted to talk with her. One of them reached through the fence and took her Sunday school paper. Kadoni opened the fence gate and took it back.

We were okay with the house on Casabonda, but we decided to move. Someone referred a house to us that was only a short distance from the Army post. It was directly across the street from a school. We could watch the students come and go. An American Army Sergeant and his family lived nearby. They had a small boy who sometimes came to play. We had electricity, water, and good plumbing. We were advised to use only drinking water from the military post. This water had gone through a purification process. My husband filled up large containers with water and brought them home. When Kadoni saw him drive up, he ran to pick up the container and carry it to the house.

As I mentioned previously, the temperature was mild. We needed neither heat nor air conditioning. The only time heat may have been needed was during the rainy season. This was because of the dampness, not because of the temperature. The second house we lived in had a fireplace. We tried it once, but it smoked up the house so much we decided not to use it. The dampness was less bothersome than the smoke.

In early fall, the PX received their toys and Christmas items. Debra's birthday is in November. We planned a birthday party for her and invited several children about her age who wanted to come. We didn't know all of them personally, but we didn't want to leave anyone out. She enjoyed the party and of course the gifts which included six identical tea sets. The PX allowed us to exchange some of the sets for other items.

The birthday party was at the NCO – Club (Non Commissioned Officers). We went there most Sundays after Chapel service. The food was very good and the wait staff was courteous and efficient. It was a pleasant treat to be able to do this.

I remember one little boy who was about Debra's age. His family was usually there every week the same time we were. He was the messiest little fellow. His food would be all over him, his face and clothes and hands. Interesting the things we remember.

As I mentioned the PX previously, we could get Christmas gifts there. We also had access to the Sears Roebuck catalog. Shipping at times could take a while. We were able to get most of what needed from the post commissary or PX. At times some of the frozen items were not so good because of being frozen for an extra long time. The gas price on post was seventeen cents a gallon.

We wrote and received mail from our family. There were no telephone calls. Email was unheard of.

There were beautiful flowers growing in many yards. There was a poinsettia in the yard across the street from our second house. It was practically a small tree, about five feet tall, and had beautiful blooms. There was a small apple tree growing in our yard. One day I saw someone climb over the fence and pick an apple. I wasn't concerned because I think it was one of the students from the school across the street from our house.

Ethiopia is a beautiful country in Northeastern Africa. There is a six hundred mile coastline bordering the Red Sea, and tall mountains inland.

Joel had an occasion to go to Massawa, one of the Red Sea ports on a short military assignment. Many of the Ethiopian people were farmers, growing a variety of crops. It was nice to drive through the countryside, and see how the local people lived. It was interesting to know that the Calla Lily is an Ethiopian lily. The Coptic Church is the official religion. Ethiopia was the home of the Biblical Queen of Sheba and King Solomon. Living there was indeed an interesting experience.

We bought several camel saddles for family members and for ourselves. The camel saddle is a stool with a cushion on top. They were made in Morocco but sold in Ethiopia. I found very comfortable and pretty shoes in the PX which were made in Italy. We bought several small containers made from an unusual wood and a surrounding insert design of porcupine quills. We also brought back a set of three small tables made with an interesting design. The little tables were made in Italy. We also brought back something else! Something special.

CHAPTER

We told Debra we were getting a baby brother or sister for her and she would then have someone to play with. I guess she was wondering why we were waking her up in the middle of the night to go and get that brother or sister.

I went to the doctor on post that day. He said it would be soon. My due date was near Joel's birthday. I didn't quite make it to that day. I woke up about two o'clock the next morning and I knew it was time.

We went to the post hospital. Joel asked a nurse to look after Debra while he helped me. This baby was in a hurry. The doctor said if my baby had come any faster, he wouldn't have been there.

A few days later, Joel brought Debra with him when he came to pick up Baby David and me. She had been staying at home with

Sarah when he came to visit. When she saw me with a baby in my arms, she turned away from me, but she quickly adjusted to him. She even let him sleep in her pink bed. She had a big girl's bed. He didn't know what color it was anyway.

When she turned four, we enrolled her in preschool at the British Embassy. Someone picked her up, along with other children, to take them to school. Sometimes, she was picked up in a horse drawn carriage. She enjoyed being with the other children. We played pretend school where I read to her and we colored pictures. Now, she could go to school with other children. They even held a graduation ceremony.

Joel advanced in rank and I think he was satisfied with the MOS-Military Occupation Specialty to which he had switched. He liked electronics and the communication process. He, of course, could not discuss his work and I did not expect him to.

David was almost one year old when Santa brought him a little car in which he could sit. See - Santa knew where to find us!

David could use his little feet to move the car all over the room, bumping into whatever was in his way. He loved doing that. Debra liked playing with her dolls and her playhouse kitchen.

As David's teeth began coming in, he wanted to bite on anything within reach. There were teeth marks on the edges of our stereo cabinet.

Joel was approaching the completion of a two and a half year assignment. I asked if we could return by ship instead of the long airplane flight and stop overs we had experienced on our way there. He said he had experienced one long uncomfortable journey on a ship. He did not want another one for himself and not for us. He remembered how many of the soldiers on the ship leaving San Francisco were sick for most of the way to Japan.

Kadoni asked Joel to bring him to the United States with us. I have thought about him many times. We didn't have time for the long process an adoption would have taken. Also, we didn't know what his family situation was. I have prayed for him and I hope the situation was what was best for him.

Completing a two and a half year assignment, it was time to move again. We were going back home! Debra was four years old, David was fifteen months.

The packing began. We moved to the post guest house to get everything ready. We would be sharing the kitchen, the laundry room, the space with other families waiting there and getting ready to leave. And, of course, getting things in and out of our traveling bags. Keeping our children occupied. Next, the rush to get everyone on the bus which would be taking us to the airport.

The bus driver took a wrong turn. We had to backtrack, barely getting to the airport in time to board before take-off. We settled in our seats, getting buckled in. An attendant came by and brought cups of milk for our children. As she gave a cup to David, he reached his little hands up and grabbed the cup. It was a plastic cup.

Squish! - milk came out, onto him, onto Mommy. It went through the front of my skirt, through the back of my skirt, on the seat. The airplane had not even left the runway. We had buckled in. All we could do was sit there.

Thank goodness, I was holding David. No milk got on Debra nor on Daddy in his uniform. We were scheduled to have a layover in Cairo, Egypt. I could change clothes in the hotel.

Nope - the only luggage we were allowed to take with us were our carry-on bags. The others would be transferred from one airplane to the other for us. We had changes of clothes for our children, but not for me.

No problem, I thought. I could get the skirt laundered at the hotel. We were to be stopping in Cairo, Egypt and staying overnight. Wrong again. No laundry facilities were available. I washed it out as best I could in the hotel bathroom sink.

The hotel in Cairo was situated beside the beautiful Nile River. We could look out our window and watch the water flow by. The room was comfortable. Our children were doing well. They really were good little travelers.

The next morning a delicious breakfast was brought to our room. We then began getting ready to board a plane again. We still had a long way to go. On the plane, we were given a front row seat. We had a generous amount of floor space, more playing area. A stewardess came by often to check on us, to ask if we needed anything and to talk with our children. She also brought toys and snacks. They seemed comfortable on the plane and cuddled up with us to nap when they got sleepy.

We traveled on, stopping to refuel in Paris, France, crossing the Atlantic Ocean, refueling again in Gander, Newfoundland, then arriving at La Guardia. We landed at La Guardia, where we began this long, interesting journey. A journey that had taken us to places I never imagined going when I married my handsome soldier. Meeting and talking with kind, friendly, generous people halfway around the world.

We went home to South Carolina to visit with our family. It was good to see them and for them to see our children. Debra had grown from a two year old to almost five. David was fifteen months old. After we visited home, we were on the road again. Back to Fort Monmouth, New Jersey.

8

CHAPTER

J oel's previous assignment at Fort Monmouth had been learning the process of electronics and communication. Now, on his return, would be teaching the process.

We moved into post housing. We were provided most of the items we needed: bedroom, living room, dining room, and furniture. Also, kitchen appliances, dishwasher, clothes washer, and dryer. Living on post was an advantage for a number of reasons.

Our neighbors had small children similar in age to Debra and David. It was good for our children to have playmates. Previously, there was rarely an opportunity to have someone other than each other or Mommy and Daddy to play with.

When Debra turned five, she went to morning preschool. A small bus picked up the children in the area. Debra remembers the way I dressed her in warm coats and boots during the winter and the trouble it was for her to take them off and put them back on again. The weather was colder in New Jersey in the winter than what we had experienced the past two and a half years. I liked seeing the snow now and then in the winter. Our children liked to play in the snow.

We were looking forward to Christmas and looking forward to something else also. I mentioned earlier that we were bringing something special with us when we left Ethiopia. Sharon Marie was born on December 26th. Debra and David had a new baby sister. Our next door neighbor looked after Debra and David and offered any other assistance we might need.

Joel took several days leave to take care of us. He did the cooking and the laundry in addition to taking care of David and Debra. We had no maid this time.

Debra and David were a little curious about their new baby sister. They quickly adjusted to having her with us.

David had a new bed. The pink bed was passed on to his baby sister.

Fortunately, I was able to stay at home with our children. I didn't have to leave them and go to work. I was thankful for that.

A few months later, my mother came to visit. Joel picked her up at the train station. It was good to see her and good for her to spend time with our children. My dad came to visit another time. It was good to have him with us also. He brought us a basket of delicious South Carolina peaches.

After a few months at Fort Monmouth it was time to move again.

9

CHAPTER

J oel was transferring to Arlington, Virginia. In New Jersey, he taught classes in electronics and communication. With this transfer to Arlington Hall he became a supervisor. The position was identified as Fixed Cryptographic Equipment Supervisor. He had advanced in rank as well.

So - we were on the road again. No military housing was available, therefore we needed to look for a place to live. Joel's brother, James, was stationed at Fort Belvoir. He and his family invited us to stay with them while we looked for a place to live.

We left New Jersey and moved in temporarily with James and his family. A little space rearrangement was needed. They did have couches and chairs. Their children were several years older than ours. So, they shared, sleeping on a couch or chair.

We met with a rental agent. He had several suggestions. He showed us a house in the neighborhood in Falls Church, Virginia. The house was near Arlington Boulevard and only a short drive to Arlington Hall. The realtor told us the house was for sale. Though we had no plans to buy a house for what would likely be a short stay, we decided to take a chance. A mortgage payment instead of a rent agreement seemed a good choice. The realtor could take care of renting the house for us when it was time to move again. The house was in a quiet neighborhood, near the elementary school. Debra would be ready for that soon. A fenced-in backyard provided a good play area for our children. We decided to buy the house. Completing that process, having our furniture delivered, getting settled, and getting familiar with his new duty station kept Joel busy.

He could handle it. He was a soldier, right?

He was assigned to Arlington Hall and on occasion, he had duty at the Pentagon. Debra was looking forward to beginning first grade in school. When we took her to register, we were told she could not begin that year. Her birthday is November the first. Their cut-off date was October 31st. They would not reason with us about that one day making the difference. She was very disappointed. We worked with her, taught her to read, and do basic math. Her daddy taught her how to tell time, how the clock works.

We liked living in Virginia. We spent time with James and Reba and their children. Ronnie, Annette, and Bobby. If we went to their house and someone happened to not be feeling well, Reba would put on a pot of potato soup. She thought that would cure whatever was ailing you. All of the children liked going to McDonalds. When we got together, this was one of the first things they brought up. Occasionally we went shopping. One day we went to Montgomery Ward's. Bobby was looking after David and he allowed him to wander off. We heard an announcement, "David Way has lost his mommy and daddy."

His name is David Ray. He was about three years old at the time, and he was having trouble with his speech. We were working with him to help improve his speech. Joel had a similar problem with his speech when he was a little boy. He wanted to help David get through it. And he did, and he learned to speak very well.

Joel received a TDY "temporary duty", assignment to Frankfurt, Germany. He was to teach a class which was scheduled to last a few weeks. He brought our children and me home to South Carolina to stay with my mother until he returned from Germany. Sharon had begun to walk. When her daddy left, she began crawling again. She seemed to be drawn to my brother, Richard, and to Joel's brother, Jack, more than she was to the women in our family. I think she was searching for Daddy.

The classes Joel and Sergeant Bolin, who would also be teaching, were delayed. The equipment they were to use was late in arrival. They were in Frankfurt to begin the classes, then transferred to Lengries to continue when the remainder of the equipment arrived. Preparing for the classes and teaching them amounted to long sessions. Joel said that the weather was not pleasant when they arrived in Germany. It was cold and raining, sleeting, or snowing much of the time. Sometimes in the evening, he and Sergeant Bolin went to a movie, or to play Bingo at the NCO club, or they went bowling. He said his luck was not always good at the Bingo table.

A short time after we arrived in South Carolina I began feeling as if I needed to see a doctor. The diagnosis confirmed my anticipation. We were going to have another baby in our family. I wrote to Joel to tell him our good news.

Joel and I wrote to each other several times a week.

In one letter he wrote, *"Honey, you don't think Sharon has forgotten me, do you?" She will probably be trying to do everything Debra and*

David do, especially David. It sounds like, from your letter, she is a lot of fun. She is learning to express herself when she is saying "no-no" in various ways. Think so? Don't let her start getting the upper hand. If she gets her way, it will encourage more of the same."

In one letter he wrote that he and Sergeant Bolin took a ski lift up the mountains near the military base. They could see a long distance of mountains and small towns from their position on the ski lift.

Joel wrote that he had taken a number of pictures and he was looking forward to showing them to me. He mailed several items homes, a music box with a small dancing doll for Debra. I don't remember what he sent to David and Sharon. He also sent several small coo-coo clocks to share with our family, two Hummel figures and a set of wall plaques with German Bavarian scenes. As you can see, he liked to collect items from different locations as he traveled.

The school Joel and the others were teaching had been intense at times. Now it was becoming more intense with exams coming up, and preparation for returning to the United States. It would be so good to have Joel home again. Our children missed their daddy. I missed him.

I assured them Daddy would be home soon. He would meet us at the train station.

I packed our bags and my brother took us to the train station there at home.

After traveling for several hours, we arrived in Virginia. They had been good little travelers and had slept part of the way. We got off the train. There was their daddy, waiting for us.

CHAPTER

As we approached our street, we heard a familiar sound. Guess what it was! The ice cream truck with music and bells announcing its arrival, just turned the corner. This became an anticipated treat for our children. When we heard the truck coming, we went outside to wait for it.

They knew they were not allowed to go out front by themselves. If they did not wait for someone to go out with them, they didn't get ice cream from the truck that day.

We had a large back yard which was fenced in across the back and both sides. Our children had a good play area there. A little boy, Kevin, about David's age lived in the house on one side of us. Several children lived in the house on the other side, though they were older.

The area was a comfortable neighborhood. Our neighbors were friendly and pleasant. There was a McDonalds not too far away. What more could one want?

Joel decided to paint the house. It was a light green. We preferred it to be white. James and Reba's son, Ronnie, was out of school for the summer. He came over and helped with the painting. Sharon liked to play with Ronnie. He taught her to play patty-cake.

As fall approached, Debra began looking forward to going to school. The school was within a short walking distance. She was ready and waiting.

She was very disappointed the first day. When we picked her up, she said, "All we did today was color." She liked her coloring books but she was ready for something else.

Our family was also ready for something else, a new addition to our family. I went to the doctors at Fort Belvoir for my regular check-up. The third week in October I had a scheduled appointment. We took Debra to school, then proceeded to James and Reba's house to drop off David and Sharon and me. Joel then went on to Arlington.

James took me to my appointment, and Reba looked after our children.

Sounds complicated, right?

The doctor said, "It won't be long."

Judging by the way I began to feel, I thought it best if I didn't go far from the Fort Belvoir hospital.

Joel picked up Debra at school and they came to James and Reba's house. She prepared supper. As she and I were cleaning up the kitchen, I felt it was time to go to the hospital. They lived only a short distance off post. It took us only a few minutes to get there.

Joel checked me in at the hospital. He was told the delivery would be a while, he could leave and come back later. He went back to James and Reba's to take care of our children, get them ready to go to bed there.

It didn't take long. A short time later, our baby Jan was born. I called Joel and he came back to the hospital. He was allowed to stay only a short time since it was already so late. He took several days leave, taking care of our children, things at home, and getting Debra to school and back. A few days later, he brought Jan and me home. The pink bed was in our room, ready and waiting for her.

Sharon and Debra shared a room and David had his room. They all adjusted well to having a new baby sister. Debra was doing very well in school. She liked going to school and her grades were excellent.

Christmastime was approaching. Santa had a list and some of

those things needed to be assembled. For instance, the scat car, the bicycle, and the play kitchen. I remember that Santa barely got everything assembled before daylight. It was worth every moment. Our children were so happy with their presents.

Springtime came. We decided to go to Washington to see the cherry trees in bloom and go to the zoo. Inside the zoo, we were looking at the monkey which had gone into space. The monkey's home was a large area behind a glass section. David and the monkey were watching each other. The monkey ran down the length of the enclosure. David ran down the length of the enclosure.

Back and forth, they did this a number of times, as though they were chasing each other. Our cute little David was having such a good time playing with the monkey. We wandered around the outside park of the large zoo, but David and the monkey are mainly what I remember, and of course the cherry trees.

David liked to watch the television show, The Adams Family. He sat in a chair and Jan was content to sit beside him in her little basket seat. Sharon watched part of the show, but when Lurch came on she ran to her room. She was afraid of Lurch. Debra didn't really care to watch. Joel had another TDY scheduled. He and some of the others at Arlington Hall were preparing to go to Lexington, Kentucky to teach other classes. Our children and I stayed home in Virginia. Joel and the others who were going to Kentucky were scheduled to be there only a few weeks. We didn't want to take Debra out of school. I assured him it would be best if our children and I remained in Virginia. James and Reba were only a short distance away if we really needed them. And - we couldn't miss the ice cream truck, could we?

One day, David and his neighborhood friend Kevin, were playing in the backyard. At least, I thought they were. I received a telephone call from a neighbor down the street, telling me that David and Kevin were riding down the middle of the street. David was in his scat car and Kevin on his scooter. Kevin's mother and I ran down the street. She took off one shoe and spanked him on his little bottom all the way back to their house. I brought David home, gave him a spanking and sent him to his room, telling him he had to stay there the rest of the day.

James and Reba came over that evening to check on us and to bring some things from the commissary. Reba was so sympathetic with David. She convinced me to allow him to come out of his room. It was a lesson learned for him. He didn't do that again!

Perhaps it was in response to me telling him how dangerous it was for him to go out in the street where he could get hurt. It may have been in response to me telling him there would be no more treats from the ice cream truck if he did that again. Also, telling him how much I love him and I did not want him to get hurt. For whatever reason, he didn't go out in the street again.

In January, Joel received an order for transfer. This time he would be going to Bangkok, Thailand. Another place neither he nor I knew much about. Moving preparations began again, but were changed when Joel was informed he could not take us with him. There was no housing available for dependents. He would have to go and report in, then secure a rental house for us. We decided our children and I would go home to South Carolina and wait until we received permission to go to Thailand.

Joel spoke with the realtor about handling the rental of our house. In their discussion, the realtor offered to buy our house. Joel decided the best option would be to sell the house to him.

We began separating what would go in storage, what would be shipped to Thailand, and what we would bring with us. Another consideration was school for Debra. She completed her first year, then summer break and began the second year. It would be a change for her wherever we were. We wanted to make the change as soon as possible. In the middle of all this, Joel spoke with someone else who received an assignment in Thailand and his family was accompanying him. So - what did Joel do?

He went directly to the Commander. The result - we were all going to Thailand.

The vaccination process began. Many vaccinations for all of us. Some members of our family thought we should not be taking our young children all over the world. Jan was fifteen months, Sharon was three, David was five, and Debra was eight.

Joel's assignment was likely to be two and a half years. Our children needed to be with their daddy. I needed to be with him, also. And he needed us.

We came home to South Carolina for a short visit with our family, then began our journey to the other side of the world.

CHAPTER

Our furniture was on the way. Our car had been taken to the port to be shipped. We were ready to board the airplane, which would take us to Travis Air Base in Oakland, California.

When we arrived at Travis, our records and passports were checked. We were told we each must get another inoculation.

We had been given so many at Fort Myer in Virginia. We were concerned that our children were getting so many, but we knew they needed the protection.

We received the boarding call and made our way to the airplane. Everyone boarding was military or dependants.

One soldier picked up Sharon. Another took Debra's hand, and someone took David's hand. They helped us get our children on the airplane.

This is what soldiers do. If a need arises, they take care of it

We boarded the plane, were assigned seats, got settled.

We were in for a long flight.

This was the first airplane trip for Sharon and Jan. David didn't remember anything about the flight from Ethiopia to the United States. He was only fifteen months old at the time. Debra remembered very little about it. She was not quite five when we returned to the United States.

Our children had toys to play with, books to read or to color. They were good little travelers.

They were curious about where we were going and why we were moving again.

Our first refueling stop was Honolulu, Hawaii. It was dark by that time, and they were asleep. They slept fairly well, all snuggled up with Daddy and me.

Joel and I were able to sleep a little also.

The next stop was Tokyo, Japan. It was daylight by then. We were served breakfast. The meals on the plane were good. Our children seemed to enjoy them.

They also enjoyed the attention they were given by the flight attendants.

There were only a few children on board.

Finally, after a seventeen hour flight, we were approaching the Bangkok airport.

We were beginning another interesting phase of an Army family's life.

Someone met us at the airport and took us to a hotel in Bangkok.

The young women who were checking us in began talking to our children. They told our little girls they liked their white hair.

They apparently didn't see many with blond hair.

The American Military facilities in Bangkok were not what we were accustomed to in the United States. STRAT COMM was located about twenty-seven miles from Bangkok in what was called Bangpla.

Other sections of the American Army were in Bangkok.

There was no housing available for those with accompanying dependants. We were to stay at the hotel while we made arrangements to rent a house.

The hotel accommodations were comfortable. There was a pleasant dining room. The food was good.

There was always rice and seafood on the lunch and dinner menu.

Our children liked most of the food that was served.

They also liked the attention they received.

There was one little glitch. Something to which we were not accustomed. Chee chucks crawled around on the ceiling of the hotel room.

Have you ever walked around a room looking up at the ceiling constantly?

That was what we felt inclined to do.

We discovered they were little geckos, which the Thai people called chee chucks. They were also convinced the little chee chucks brought good luck. Therefore, they all wanted them in their house, also in the hotel.

Eventually we learned to accept them. We began looking for a house to rent. We found one, which seemed adequate, met the owner, and agreed on a rent charge.

We were ready to move in, then received troubling news.

There had been a warehouse fire and our stored items were damaged or destroyed.

The little pink bed was one of the destroyed items.

We went through a long process of remembering and listing the items which were damaged or destroyed. We were reimbursed.

We bought Jan another little bed. She didn't seem to mind that she no longer had the pink one in which to sleep.

The house we rented was comfortable. There was a spacious yard surrounded by a strong concrete and brick fence and a gate with a lock.

Our children had a good, safe playing area.

The owner came frequently and brought a young man who cut the grass as well as other yard work.

There were many flowers growing in the yard. She wanted to make certain they were taken care of.

Occasionally, she brought various kinds of fruit for us.

Several interesting and delicious fruits were grown there. For example, there was pineapple, mango, pomelo, papaya and several others.

We enrolled Debra and David in a small private school. There was a large international elementary through high school where English was taught.

We decided the small school would be better for our children. We thought they would be more comfortable in the smaller school.

David was beginning first grade, and Debra was third grade level.

English was taught. There were students from a number of countries. Many of the parents were with the Embassy or the American Military.

Classes were first through seventh grade. The school schedule was three months of classes, one month off, then three more of classes.

This totaled one grade of school. During the two and a half years we were in Thailand, our children were able to advance an extra grade from where they would have been in the United States.

There was only one other student in Debra's grade level. They became good friends. She came to visit after we returned to the United States.

Living in Thailand created many new experiences for us.

For example, my first ride to the commissary was interesting. One day while we were at the hotel, I decided to go to the commissary.

There was always a taxi nearby. I asked someone at the hotel to flag one for me and to tell the driver where I wanted to go, just in case he did not understand or speak English.

I discovered the driver did understand and speak English.

We went in and out one street after another before arriving at the commissary.

I was expecting an outrageous amount he would tell me I owed him because of the distance and the time involved in getting there.

He surprised me when he asked if I would get apples for him instead of paying him for the ride.

He waited for me and returned me to the hotel.

As I mentioned previously, all the delicious fruits grown there. Apples were not usually available.

Another interesting occurrence - one morning I opened the outside door leading to the patio.

As I leaned over to hook the latch, another surprise was waiting. A huge cobra, and I mean huge, was curled up on the patio, apparently enjoying the morning sunshine.

It was the largest cobra I had ever seen and was an interesting yellow color.

I backed up slowly and watched the cobra slither away.

There was a khlong a short distance from the house. I assumed that was where it came from and stopped by for a nap on our warm and sunny porch.

I was thankful our children were not in the yard.

Chee chucks, monkeys, cobra - a lot to get accustomed to

- And more yet to come!

CHAPTER

T he people living in the house next to us made silk fabric. Their looms were outside in a covered, though open, section of their house.

The process was interesting to watch, and the results were beautiful.

Another interesting thing about our neighbors occurred one evening.

We heard the sound of unusual music. When we looked outside, we saw several people dancing in the yard.

They were dressed in colorful clothing, and the women wore beautiful headware.

The dancers could have been practicing for a performance, or they were simply having a good time.

Our children enjoyed playing outside. The weather was warm and comfortable. We left Virginia in January, when the weather was quite cold.

We decided to get an inflatable pool for them to play in. It was too small to be called a swimming pool.

They had fun playing in the water. Never mind swimming.

There was a beautiful bougainvillea growing by the back porch, climbing up and over the top of the back door. Butterflies frequently flew in and out of the plant.

Our children liked the butterflies. Something else our children liked to see was the water delivery truck.

The truck brought bottles of water, and also it brought something special, orange and grape Fanta sodas. Those were a treat for our children.

We were advised not to drink the local water. It was good to be able to have the bottled water delivered.

There were large, beautiful Buddhist temples. Many of the Thai people are Buddhist.

We occasionally saw a monk walk by. They were easily recognized by the orange robes they wore.

We discovered there was a missionary from the United States who held Sunday morning worship services in a large assembly room at a hotel in Bangkok.

He was from Greenville, South Carolina. We attended the Sunday morning worship services there at the hotel.

They didn't have Sunday School. We read Bible stories to our children at home and talked to them about Jesus.

Debra and David were doing well at school. A van came and picked them up, then brought them back each day.

I didn't drive in Thailand. There seemed to be no traffic restrictions. Cars, trucks, buses, double-seated carts, bicycles. They all assumed the right of way.

Joel was comfortable driving, right long with them. If I needed to go some place and he wasn't at home to take me, a taxi was always available.

Occasionally, on the weekend, we went for a ride in the area surrounding Bangkok.

It was interesting to explore the area. We saw rice farmers working with water buffalo.

Occasionally, we saw an elephant carrying a heavy load of tree trunks and limbs. After the trees were cut, elephants carried them strapped on their back to factories where they were then processed.

The wood from the trees such as bamboo, teak, monkey pod was used to make beautiful useful items.

We bought several things made from different types of wood.

For example - two large floor lamps, a round table with four matching stools.

Each of the stools had a cushion with a removable cover. We have vases made from wood with interesting designs, a servicing set with a large bowl and small ones.

Each piece is shaped like half a pineapple. They were carved from monkey pod wood.

The pieces are washable. They are used to serve fruit or salad.

We toured a large firestone factory where tires were made from a mixture using wood from rubber trees.

Someone there gave us a small ashtray shaped like a tire.

I didn't realize there were so many different types of trees and used for such different items.

People in Thailand enjoyed making and flying kites. They made large kites with faces and interesting designs in a variety of shapes.

The kites had long strings which allowed them to fly high in the sky and swoop all around.

There were contests at times to determine who had the biggest and the best kite.

Sharon was afraid of those kites. When she saw them swooping around, she wanted nothing to do with them.

There are many interesting traditions. For example, they celebrate the new year by throwing water on each other.

This is called Songkran and is done to say Happy New Year.

Our children thought this was a fun thing to do.

Another celebration is observed because of the rainy season. For many months, there is little rain. Then there is almost constant rain for several weeks.

When the rains stop, they celebrate. This is called Loi Krathong.

The people make little boats from banana tree leaves.

They fill the little boats with flowers and candles, then light the candles and release the boats to float down the khlong.

The khlongs are used for many reasons. For example, people travel from one place to another in small boats.

They anchor, then buy and sell different items. This is called the floating market.

We occasionally went to what was called the Saturday market. The vendors sold a variety of items, including food, clothing, toys, jewelry and silk.

There was always something of interest for our children.

A Christmas party was planned at the hotel where some of the

American Military offices were. Our children were excited about going to see Santa Claus. They started making their lists for Santa.

We also talked with them about the real special reason for celebrating Christmas, the birth of Jesus.

I don't know how excited Jan was when Santa picked her up and they were face to face.

She had a really doubtful look on her little face. It was like she was thinking "Who are you?"

Her daddy took her picture with Santa.

Refreshments were served, and the children played games. They all received a bag of candy from Santa.

Joel introduced me to someone with whom he worked.

The man raised his eyebrows and said to Joel, "This is yours?"

I assume that was a compliment.

13
CHAPTER

We decided to move to a different section of Bangkok, which was closer to Bangpla. This would make Joel's drive each day a little shorter.

The street was Soi 81, which meant street number 81, off Sukhumvit. This was the highway Joel traveled each day.

The house had a living room, kitchen, dining area on the ground floor. The bedrooms were upstairs.

There was a section for the maid adjoining the back side of the house.

The yard was spacious and was surrounded by the usual concrete wall and sturdy fence gate.

Speaking of the maid, she always addressed Joel and me as master and madam. She was kind and caring with our children.

If I had errands or appointments, I knew she would take care of them. I didn't have many errands or appointments, though I knew when I did have, I could depend on her.

One day I returned from some place, most likely the commissary. She was very upset. She said "Madam, madam, Master David, he-he..." She kept repeating what she was trying to say to me.

Our children had a record player, and they used it frequently. There was a little mishap that day.

The record player was electric. They were supposed to use it when there was supervision.

The electric power there was 50 watt, while the little record player was 60 watt.

We had adapters to take care of this. The record player had been connected without the adapter. It wasn't working.

David tried to fix it with one of his daddy's screwdrivers. Instead of fixing it, he punched a hole in it.

The little record player still worked when it was plugged in correctly, even with a little hole in it.

David learned a lesson that day, and thankfully no one was hurt.

As I mentioned previously, the yard was surrounded by a

substantial fence. Our children had a good size safe area in which to play.

There were banana and mango trees in the yard. They produced delicious fruit.

The family living on one side of us raised orchids. We could see there were many of the beautiful plants growing.

The owner gave us one of the orchids as a welcoming gift. We placed it on a plant hanger in the yard.

When we were outside, we frequently saw big airplanes flying across the sky. Many of them were B52 bombers.

There was an American Air Base south of Bangkok. The B52s were going to and from Vietnam.

To our children, they were simply big airplanes. They had no idea of the seriousness of their missions.

Just as they had no idea of the seriousness of their daddy's duties.

He was the Strategic Communications Command Station Chief there in Bangkok.

He was presented The First Oak Leaf Cluster to the Army Commendation Medal while he was there.

We didn't know at the time that this information was sent to our hometown newspaper.

My mother sent us a copy of the article from her newspaper. I would like to share it with you.

Sergeant First Class Joel R. Ledford, presently serving in Thailand, recently received The First Oak Leaf Cluster to The Army Commendation Medal. The award was presented for meritorious service in the Army while Sergeant Ledford was assigned to The U.S. Army Strategic Communications Command at Arlington Hall, Virginia.

He was Fixed Cryptograph Equipment Supervisor and contributed to the introduction of new electronic equipment to Army activities throughout the world.

Sergeant Ledford previously received the Purple Heart and the Army Commendation Medal in addition to other awards.

Joel had two TDY assignments while he was in Bangkok. Thankfully, neither was as long as the one to Germany had been.

He went to Okinawa for about three weeks. Several months later, he went to Hawaii for about the same length of time.

He always brought a surprise when he returned.

I don't remember what he brought for our children on the assignment to Okinawa.

I do remember the intricately designed glass bowl with several fruit shaped pieces of the same glass material.

From Hawaii, he brought our three daughters each a pretty little Hawaii doll. He brought David a G.I. Joe.

Sometime later, our children were playing in the yard when someone reached through the fence gate and took the G.I. Joe from David.

However, he didn't get to keep it. Someone made him give it back to David.

Our daughters still have those little Hawaii dolls.

I was a member of the NCO Wive's Club. I was chosen to be president for a six month period.

Thinking of something different and interesting to do, I spoke with the manager of a women's clothing store.

I asked if she would bring some of the clothing items to one of our meetings. She kindly agreed to do so.

I thought she would model them for us.

No - it didn't happen that way. She asked me to model the items, which she brought from the store, while she described them.

I did so, and I guess I did okay. They were beautiful clothes, made in a variety of designs and colors.

I considered the modeling a lesson learned. Be careful what you ask for.

My mother would have thought that was an interesting

experience. She worked at a women's clothing store back home in South Carolina.

Thinking of my mother brings back memories of the many times I just wished I could see her, talk with her, be with her.

Our correspondence was by mail. I couldn't just pick up a telephone and call when I was half way around the world away from her.

We had telephone service, but it didn't reach across an ocean and a continent.

We did have air mail. We also had television service on a limited basis with a little antenna on top of the television.

Joel's change in assignment was drawing near. We began preparing to leave Thailand and return to the United States.

I decided to make new dresses for our daughters to wear on the plane. I bought David new pants and shirt. Boys clothes seemed a little more difficult to make, at least for me.

My sewing machine had been destroyed in the warehouse fire. We bought a new one at the P.X.

We began sorting and packing and getting ready to leave. I went to school to get Debra and David's records.

We were leaving in July. They would have a few weeks before beginning a new school year when we reached the United States.

Joel sold our car to someone who worked at the Embassy there.

We went to the airport. We had to wait a long time. I don't know why the long delay.

We were assigned a hotel room, ate supper, then a short sleep time, got up in the middle of the night to return to the airport.

As we boarded the airplane, music was playing "We are going to San Francisco."

As the others came on the plane, they responded to the music – "We are trying. We are trying."

We settled in. Our children went to sleep.

We were going home.

CHAPTER

Our first refueling stop was Manila. Someone came on the plane and gave each of us a delicious orange.

After refueling and enjoying the oranges, we were on our way again.

We arrived in California after many hours in the air. A short time later, we were on another airplane on the way to South Carolina.

Our children probably thought "When are we ever getting off this airplane?"

We finally arrived in South Carolina. It was so good to see and spend time with my mother, my dad, my brother and Joel's family.

Joel had requested several weeks leave time before reporting to his duty station.

This gave our children time to get to know their grandparents and other members of our family again. They had grown a bit during the two and a half years we were away.

Debra, David and Sharon remembered them, though I don't think Jan did. They probably enjoyed the attention they received.

We needed transportation. Joel began looking for a car to replace the one he sold before we left Thailand.

He bought a yellow Chrysler. Our children loved the new car. I think they liked the yellow color.

We enjoyed our time at home in South Carolina. My husband's leave time went by too quickly. It was good to be able to spend time with our family, but we had to get on the road again.

We had a long way to go. Joel's next duty assignment was California.

This would definitely be another long trip, by automobile this time, not by airplane.

We packed our bags, told our family goodbye. We were on our way.

Joel decided to take the northern route, moving west. Leaving South Carolina, we drove through the beautiful green countryside of Western Northern Carolina and Tennessee mountains.

We merged with Interstate 40, which took us the rest of the way to California.

Our children played with toys, read books and comics and colored page after page.

They came up with something different to do also. They began making a list of all the different state license plates they saw on automobiles between South Carolina and California.

They were able to complete a long list.

As we traveled, we made several stops along the way so our children could get out of the car.

We stopped to get lunch or ice cream, to look at something interesting or to just walk for a bit.

Late evening, we began looking for a motel and a place to get supper. The first night, we stayed at a motel called The Travelodge.

Our children liked that one because of the advertising symbol. They called it the "Sleepy Bear" motel, because of the sign with a bear cuddled up with a blanket.

I liked it because it was comfortable, though the little bear was cute.

Before continuing our journey each morning, we ate breakfast at the motel. We then got in the car, settled in, and we were on our way.

About halfway to California, we had to take an unexpected side trip. The air conditioning in the car stopped working.

This was the air conditioning in our new car!

Unexpected occurrences do happen.

We took an exit and located a repair shop. The problem was taken care of.

As evening approached, our children began looking for the Sleepy Bear.

After five days on the road, we arrived in San Francisco in the evening. We spent the first night in a hotel.

Joel reported in the next morning. His duty station was Fort Baker, which was across The Golden Gate Bridge from the Presidio.

We would be living at the Presidio. We checked in the post guest house to stay until our furniture arrived and living quarters were ready for us.

That night, we heard an unusual sound outside. We looked out to see what it was. Several raccoons were rummaging in the garbage containers.

They were not bothering anyone or anything. They were just looking for food.

We stayed at the guest house for several days. It was comfortable. We shared the kitchen and dining area with others who were staying there.

There was a playground for the children. After a few days, we were assigned a house. Our furniture was delivered. We moved in.

I remember the address – 758A Portola Street. The house was a brick two-story with a large basement, sidewalks along the street in the front, a nice backyard.

Living on post was good for a number of reasons.

Fort Baker was a short drive over the Golden Gate Bridge each morning and evening for my husband.

We could see the bridge from an upstairs window clearly if the fog didn't have it covered. At times, the fog was extremely heavy. We heard the fog horns frequently, especially at night.

Another experience one night was a mild tremor of the house, not enough to cause any damage. We were thankful for that.

That was the only occurrence of anything of that nature we experienced while we were in San Francisco.

It was mid-summer when we moved to California. It would be several weeks before school began.

With not being required to begin school immediately, our children had a little time to become adjusted to our surroundings.

They met some of the other children in the neighborhood. A family with a little girl about Sharon's age lived across the street from us. Her name was Freida. They began playing together and chasing butterflies.

There were many Monarch Butterflies in the area. The girls would catch them in a net, then release them and watch as they flew away.

We did a little research about the Monarchs. We read that they come from Mexico, fly up through California, then continue across the United States to the northeastern section of this country.

Our children decided to take swimming lessons. Instruction was given at a large indoor pool on post.

When Sharon's height was measured, she was one inch shorter than the required limit.

An exception was made. She was allowed to take the lessons because her brother and her sister would be there with her. The instructor looked after her also.

She learned to be a good little swimmer.

Jan was too little to take the lessons. She didn't want to take them anyway.

She was satisfied staying home. I had a birthday coming up, and I received a surprise with it.

Debra wanted to do something special for me and had talked with her daddy about it.

She and I went to the post theater, just the two of us, to see the movie "Around the World in Eighty Days" with David Niven in the lead role. Debra was so pleased to take me to a movie.

She was also pleased to take Jan to the post library for reading hour and to check out books, and of course a quick stop at the PX to get hot chocolate sometimes.

One little problem occurred one day. Jan burned her tongue on the hot chocolate. It wasn't too bad though. She was happy to be allowed to go with her sister.

September arrived, time for Debra and David to begin school again.

Sharon was five years old, and Jan was three. They would be staying at home with Mommy.

There was no school for children on post, but there was an excellent school, Winfield Scott, very near the post gate.

Going to a new school was not really a problem for them. They adjusted well to a much larger school than the previous one they attended in Thailand.

A bus picked up our children and others along the way and drove them to the post gate. From there, someone walked with them in a line the short distance to school.

As they walked past The Palace of Fine Arts, they enjoyed stopping to watch the white swans in a pond of water there.

15

CHAPTER

One weekend, we decided to do a little exploring.

Lombard Street in San Francisco is famous for its winding design. We went to check it out. If my memory is correct, the street is made from brick.

As we began our drive on Lombard, someone dressed like Santa Claus was driving a red car, and came around us.

It was not Christmas, but the Santa was in a hurry for some reason.

We then rode over the Golden Gate Bridge to Sausalito. We went to a toy store, a furniture store and several other places.

We had a good day just checking things out.

Another exciting day was coming up. Actually, I should say evening. Our children were getting ready for Halloween.

Sharon remembers wearing a Cinderella outfit.

There were numerous children at our door that evening. We gave out a lot of candy. Our children brought home as much as we gave away.

They enjoyed being able to do this. Debra and David did other interesting things with their school classmates.

David's class made a visit to Coit Tower, a tall building in San Francisco. He liked looking out the windows of the tall building and seeing the ground below.

Debra's class went to Fisherman's Wharf and to an appearance by the San Francisco Symphony.

They were both doing well in school.

Christmas time. Santa had not lost us in the many times we moved from one state or one country to another.

On Christmas morning our girls were enjoying their gifts, which included Beatles records for their record player.

David and his dad were down on the floor putting together a race car track.

I called my mother. It was so good to hear her voice.

At times, on these long deployments, so many miles away, I just wished I could see my mother, talk with her, spend time with her and my brother Richard.

We continued to write letters to each other, but that was not as close as person to person. I was thankful my brother was with her.

Spring came. We decided to go to Disneyland one weekend. We left the Presidio on a Saturday morning, then drove South from San Francisco to San Diego, then on to Disneyland.

We saw the large Hollywood letters on a hillside as we passed by.

After checking into the El Toro Marine Base guesthouse, we ate lunch, then went to Disneyland.

Our children enjoyed participating in many of the games, rides and events.

They especially liked "It's a Small World." We sat in the small boats that traveled through the water.

The music "It's a Small World" continued to play. Different scenes, numerous items appeared around us as the little boats moved along.

These items and images represented countries around the world.

We went to the El Toro guesthouse to spend the night, then we went back to Disneyland the following morning.

I was given a pretty corsage, which was a pleasant surprise. It happened to be Mother's Day.

Afternoon came, time to get back on the road. We had another long ride ahead of us.

The following day was Monday. Back to work for Daddy, back to school for Debra and David.

They were both doing well in school. Summer break would be coming soon.

Our children enjoyed being outside. The weather was usually comfortable. They could get together with their friends.

Something else they enjoyed was playing on the narrow beach along San Francisco Bay.

The commissary parking lot extended very close to the big rocks on the beach.

Sometimes Joel would drop me off at the commissary, and he would go with them to play on the rocks and feed the seagulls.

I have a sweet picture of our children there on the rocks. The Golden Gate Bridge can be seen in the background.

Joel left from this harbor on a troop ship, beginning a journey across the Pacific Ocean twenty years earlier.

My prayers for his safe return were answered.

Then, twenty years later, he was sitting on the rocks along the bay with his four precious children, tossing crumbs to seagulls. Something he never imagined happening.

He decided to do something else in the Pacific Ocean - fishing.

A young boy named Brian and his family lived next door to us. He and David were about the same age, eight. Joel and Sergeant Bell decided one weekend to secure space on a fishing boat for Brian, David and themselves.

The boat went a short distance into the Pacific Ocean.

Not many fish were caught that day, but guess who did catch fish.

David and Brian each caught a fish that day, and they were big fish.

The boys received a little help from their dads reeling the fish in. They really were big fish. We have photographs to prove it.

The boys were so excited. Something else exciting was coming up. My dad and his wife, Ila, were coming for a visit.

My dad was a baseball fan and his favorite team, the Atlanta Braves, was scheduled to play at Candlestick Park.

We planned to make certain he went to the game. We also wanted them to see some of California while they were with us.

Joel took several days leave. School was out for summer.

So, ball game first. We loaded up and went to Candlestick Park. There were a number of people there as we expected. We were able to get good seating. That was nice.

My dad appreciated the opportunity to attend the game. It was a pleasure for us for him to have that opportunity.

He bought a gift for each of our children, a baseball or a toy of some kind.

They liked the gift more than they did the ball game. They did like going to Candlestick Park. They thought that was a funny name.

One day, we went to the NCO club for lunch. I thought everyone might want something different from my cooking.

We wanted my dad and Ila to see some of San Francisco. We took them for a ride on Lombard Street, over the Golden Gate Bridge, to Sausalito, to Sonoma, across the Oakland Bridge, to other places of interest.

They thought Fisherman's Wharf was interesting. They didn't care to take any streetcar rides.

We had another visitor a short time later. My husband's nephew, Ron, was in the Air Force and was stationed in Okinawa.

He came through San Francisco and stopped to see us. He was on leave and was going home to Virginia.

Ron brought a gift, a set of a glass bowl and fruit, similar to the set Joel brought back from a TDY to Okinawa when we were in Thailand.

Ron continued to serve, and several years later, he retired from the Air Force.

Jan woke up one morning with an earache. Joel took us to the

Letterman, the post hospital to see a doctor. He went to Fort Baker to check in, then returned to Letterman.

The doctor took care of Jan immediately. He was gentle with her. She was not fussy. She was quiet and did what he instructed her to do.

As we were leaving, one of the men on duty there made a rude remark to a coworker that our little girl was not really sick, she just wanted attention.

It was obvious he intended for me to hear what he said.

I was upset when I returned to the car, and I told Joel what the man said.

My husband parked the car, went inside and gave the man a few words of advice.

I can only imagine what those words were!

As I write, my thoughts often wander. I think about the different places my husband has served. The many places we have taken our children.

Many hours, many miles, in an automobile or an airplane. How they adapted to different climates, different cultures, different languages.

As I mentioned earlier, home for them was wherever their daddy was.

CHAPTER

I knew my husband's service was electronics and communications, though I knew very little of the details.

He had gone from infantry, supply, recruiting, then strategic communication.

He was awarded the Purple Heart and a number of other commendations.

Sergeant Bell contacted me to tell me Joel was to be presented another commendation, and I was invited to attend.

Joel was not aware of the scheduled commendation nor my invitation.

Sergeant Bell asked Mrs. Bell to look after our children.

A number of the men who were assigned there were in the room to attend the presentation.

When Joel came into the room, he was surprised to see me there. He probably thought "What is my wife doing here, and where are our children?"

Joel had come a long way from recruit to Master Sergeant, and was then Station Chief at Fort Baker.

I was very proud of my husband.

A historical event occurred while we were in San Francisco. On July 20, 1969, three astronauts, Neil Armstrong, Buzz Aldrin, and Michael Collins landed the Apollo spaceship on the moon. Neil Armstrong was the first man on the moon.

Our children found this interesting, and they wanted to know how a man could walk on the moon. They wanted to know more about it.

The fall session of school began. Sharon was happy that she and her brother would be going to school together at Winfield Scott.

Debra began her first year at Junior High. She rode the city bus to Marina Junior High.

Jan was left at home again. Her time for school would come later. She had a birthday coming up in October. She would then be five.

We planned a party for her. Several children in the neighborhood were invited.

We had birthday parties for her brother and her sisters. This was her first birthday party where other children came. That was special for her.

Another party was planned. A Hawaiian Luau. The mess hall staff prepared a special meal. They even roasted a pig. There was beautiful Hawaiian music in the background.

My husband had a lot on his mind and a major decision to make. The Hawaiian dinner was a welcome diversion.

He was nearing the completion of twenty-one years of military service.

He had advanced in rank from recruit to Master Sergeant. One more step to the top of the ladder. Sergeant Major.

Did he want to continue for that or was he ready to retire.

We were discussing this one evening after our children had gone to bed.

We heard an unusual sound, like numerous drums. We discovered those sounds were coming from Alcatraz, an island out some distance in the Pacific Ocean.

Alcatraz had been a prison there in the ocean, but was no longer occupied as such.

It had become inhabited by protestors. I don't know exactly what they were protesting, but they were beating those drums loud enough to be heard across the Bay to San Francisco quite a distance away.

Back to the issue, my husband and I were discussing. He knew I supported whatever decision he chose.

He enlisted in the United States Army when he was a teenager. For the next twenty-one years he traveled the world. Was he ready to give that up? He had one year of college. Did he want to continue in college? What kind of work did he want to do?

He was very knowledgeable in electronics. Maybe something in that line would be a possibility.

After much consideration, he decided to retire, give our children a chance to settle down, move home to South Carolina.

Living at the Presidio was an interesting experience. It was a comfortable, well-organized military base with a long history.

The Presidio was considered the United States Army's premier West Coast location, a military post of exceptional significance in the American West.

It is bordered on the west by waters of the Pacific Ocean, on the north by the San Francisco Bay, on the south and east by the urban landscape of San Francisco.

The Golden Gate Bridge is a beautiful and interesting bridge. Construction of the bridge began in 1933 and was completed in 1937.

The Presidio tells the story of the development of the Western United States and guards one of the world's finest natural harbors.

It reflects more than two hundred years of military history served under three flags.

From 1761 to 1821 under Spanish rule, American military obtained control in 1848 and ruled the area until 1994.

From 1941 until 1945, the Presidio served as a major training center for Army troops headed for the World War II Pacific Theater.

1964 until 1973, Southeast Asia bound troops arrived and left from the Presidio. Plans were made to move the US Army troops and to close the military base.

The National Park Service was scheduled to take over the location.

Congress passed the Base Closure Bill in 1988, and the Presidio was scheduled for decommissioning.

In 1994, the Sixth Army left and the Presidio officially became part of the National Park Service.

We were at the Presidio from 1967 until 1969.

My husband submitted his resignation. We began our moving plans.

We couldn't take everything in the trunk of our car this time, as we did when we began this journey.

We were due to leave about the end of November.

We would decide what to take with us. The movers would take care of the rest.

Our plan was to go home to South Carolina, then decide where to go from there.

There were a number of things on our "to do" list before we reached that point.

Thanksgiving was coming. I needed to plan dinner and prepare for that. I decided to keep it simple.

We received a surprise. Sergeant and Mrs. Bell brought lunch to us. Also, for some reason, Sergeant Bell thought Jan would like to have a turkey leg.

It was a big turkey leg. She shared most of it, only eating a small amount of it herself.

The Bells were kind, thoughtful people, good neighbors to have.

Back to the moving plan. When we had the sorting, packing, cleaning done, we checked in the post guest house. We stayed there several days, taking care of last minute details.

We decided to take the Southern route on our return to South Carolina to see other parts of our country, and while we were in California, why not go to Disneyland again?

That was what we did, went to Disneyland.

We left the Scott Hall guest house at the Presidio on a Friday morning, took Highway 1, continued on Highway 5 going south.

We saw orchard after orchard of orange trees loaded with oranges.

Continuing on to Anaheim, we stayed at the El Toro Marine base to spend the night at the guest house.

The following morning, we left El Toro and went to Disneyland.

After a busy day at Disneyland, our children were happy to find a "Sleepy Bear" motel.

Joel and I were ready for a break also.

After a good night's sleep, we were on the road again. Arizona was next on our route.

We stopped for lunch and to walk around. We went into a game shop. They had a wide variety of games and rocks. Our children each chose one for a souvenir.

The following day, we were driving through New Mexico. When we stopped for lunch, I ordered something I had not eaten before, a TACO. I was surprised how good it was.

After New Mexico, Texas was next. As we rode through Texas, we saw mile after mile of oil rigs and turbines. Our children were interested in how they operated.

We continued on through Louisiana, Mississippi, Alabama, then northeast through Georgia.

After five days, covering more than two thousand miles, we were nearing South Carolina.

When we arrived in South Carlina, we went to my mother's house. We would stay with her until we decided what our next step would be.

Over the next several days, we visited with my dad, my brother, and Joel's family.

It was good to see everyone and to be home again.

CHAPTER

J oel's brother Calvin told him about a new housing development. He had helped the owners with the auction of the land and had purchased three adjoining lots from the sellers.

He and Joel went to look at the property. He offered to sell the three lots to Joel for the amount he paid for them.

Joel liked the location, the area, and the size of the lots. He accepted Calvin's offer.

A street had been cut and paved through the area. The lots were about an acre each. Numerous trees were on the property. Some of them had been cut down.

My dad was a carpenter, a very knowledgeable builder. We asked if he would build a house for us. He willinging accepted.

My mother kindly allowed us to stay with her while the building was being done.

In the meantime, we had enrolled our children in school. Sharon and David were in elementary, and Debra was in Junior High.

They adapted well to the new schools.

Joel helped my dad and his crew. He said he was their "go-for" person. He picked up supplies for them.

Construction was not his specialty. When our new house was finished, we notified the storage facility to deliver our furniture and other items.

We did not have many furniture items. Most of the places we lived off post were adequately furnished.

When we lived on post, all we had to do was request the items we needed and delivery would be arranged.

So, we went furniture shopping. David did not care what the furniture looked like. He wanted an orange rug and orange bed covers.

This was before he knew that much if anything about Clemson Football.

We were so excited to move into our new house. The first night there we toasted with cups of grape juice.

Our children snuggled up in their new beds. Debra had her own room. David had his, along with his orange accessories.

Sharon and Jan shared a room with twin beds.

My dad received another job offer. Joel's brother Jack bought one of the three property lots and asked my Dad to build a house for him.

My dad agreed to do so. He was accustomed to bringing his lunch from home when he was on a job.

I invited him to eat lunch with us, and he did, but he continued to bring his lunch from home.

Guess why?

Jan loved to share Grandpa's lunch with him. He didn't want to disappoint her, so he continued to bring lunch.

Jan also liked to help her grandpa with his work.

Her brother and her sisters were in school, and she still could not go.

With my dad building the house on one of the lots next-door, he was nearby working.

He let Jan sit in the bed of his truck when it was safe to do so.

She thought she was helping him. After the house building was finished, my husband went to work repairing televisions.

In addition to doing that, he was teaching me to drive.

As I mentioned previously, the driving habits in some of the places we lived was not something I wanted to compete with.

David asked his dad one day, "Why does mom drive around the road with the brake light on?"

I was just being cautious! Joel decided to build a television when he was not doing repairs. He ordered the instruction books and there were a number of them, from Bell & Howell.

He also ordered the equipment and the parts to build the television and a wood cabinet for it.

Joel began studying the instructions. Then he and David began putting the television together.

In their construction process, Joel read the instructions, then showed David where the part fit and how to attach it.

David did a good bit of the building process with his dad's assistance.

The television was a large floor model. They did an excellent job with it, and I think they both learned a lot in the process.

David enjoyed building the television with his dad.

Joel wanted David to have that learning experience and he enjoyed doing it with David.

We all enjoyed the television. Joel repaired televisions for several months. He wanted something different to do.

There were only three Radio Shack stores in South Carolina. One was in Charleston, one in Columbia, and the third was in the final state of completion in Greenville.

Mr. Tandy owned the company. He was offering an interesting opportunity for new store managers.

And of course, this would expand the operation of Radio Shack.

The proposal was called SMIA - Special Manager Incentive Agreement.

Joel was interested in obtaining more information.

He contacted the District manager to discuss details. Joel told him that he wanted to investigate further before making a decision.

He contacted the other South Carolina Radio Shack managers and discussed the details of the SMIA agreement.

Becoming a Radio Shack owner/manager seemed to be what Joel was looking for.

He called the district manager and gave him his decision. The district manager asked Joel to look for a suitable location.

Joel checked out several spaces. A Western Auto had recently opened. There were four spaces in addition to Western Auto in the strip. Three of those were occupied, one vacant, just waiting for us.

This did seem to be a good location with other businesses,

including a post office, a book store, a restaurant, and automobile dealership in the vicinity and another line of various stores nearby.

An interesting coincidence, my brother Richard worked at the automobile dealership. It was just across the street from where Radio Shack would be located.

The district manager came to sign the contract agreement.

Furnishings for the store were delivered - cabinets, display cases, operating equipment.

These were installed and the merchandise arrived. Stereos, speakers, radios, telephones, capacitors, resistors, transistors, I could go on and on. I had no idea what many of the items were. The Boss knew. That was what was important.

I did have a job. I was to be the accountant. I could do that.

My husband had not lost his traveling companion.

I went to work with him each morning, then home with him each night.

EPILOGUE

I was nineteen when I married my handsome soldier, and we began our journey together.

As the song goes, "When I fall in love, it will be forever."

There was something special about Joel. I believe meeting was meant to be. I believe God brought him to me.

The same is true of our children. Each one has a special place in my heart and was a gift from God.

As I write these words, I can see our children in all steps of their lives, how they accepted and adapted to the moving from one place to another.

We were fortunate to be living those experiences, being able to travel with their daddy as much as we did.

Being a military wife is not for everyone, but definitely being able to turn to God in a time of need is crucial. He is in control.

When we acknowledge this, we are able to adjust to changing situations with more confidence.

Our trust in God enables us to overcome any fears that may be dormant as we go about our daily lives.

When our husband is deployed and we cannot go with him, we can carry on until he returns.

Once at a writer's conference, I heard a woman make a comment about a decision she forced her husband to make.

She gave him an ultimatum, his choice, her or the Navy.

I don't know which he chose, but it was obvious she regretted what she had done.

There are at times issues with military service, but also there are commitments, which must be honored and obeyed.

For a period of time after my husband retired, we missed the military life. The connection was still there.

We settled in, busy with work for Joel and me, school for the children.

Our children grew up too quickly. They graduated high school and college.

It was good having them work with us at Radio Shack.

They had plans other than Radio Shack for their future. Debra and Sharon became school teachers. Jan is a court reporter. David is a Baptist minister.

Their dad and I have always been proud of them.

I dedicate this book to our children:

Debra – David – Sharon – Jan, and to our grandchildren.

To Joel, I say, "Thank you for the memories."

Printed in the United States
by Baker & Taylor Publisher Services